KAIFI&I

— A MEMOIR —

KAIFI & I

── A MEMOIR ──

SHAUKAT KAIFI

Edited & Translated by Nasreen Rehman

zubaan

ZUBAAN
an imprint of Kali for Women
128 B Shahpur Jat, 1st floor
NEW DELHI 110 049
Email: zubaan@gmail.com and zubaanwbooks@vsnl.net
Website: www.zubaanbooks.com

First published in English (2010) by Zubaan

10 9 8 7 6 5 4 3 2

ISBN   978 81 89013 75 2

Zubaan is an independent feminist publishing house based in New Delhi with
a strong academic and general list. It was set up as an imprint of India's first
feminist publishing house, Kali for Women, and carries forward Kali's tradition
of publishing world quality books to high editorial and production standards.
Zubaan means tongue, voice, language, speech in Hindustani. Zubaan is a non-
profit publisher, working in the areas of the humanities, social sciences, as well as
in fiction, general non-fiction, and books children and for young adults under its
Young Zubaan imprint.

Typeset by Jojy Philip, New Delhi 110 015
Printed at Raj Press, R-3 Inderpuri, New Delhi 110 012

For Shabana and Baba

Contents

Acknowledgments		ix
Introduction: *Ralph Russell*		1
Foreword: *Priyamvada Gopal*		6
Translator's Note: *Nasreen Rehman*		13
1.	Growing up in Hyderabad	17
2.	Making My Own Choices	33
3.	Living in a Commune	41
4.	In Search of a Home	58
5.	Heartache and Fulfilment	66
6.	Red Flag Hall	77
7.	Treading the Boards	86
8.	The Silver Screen	101
9.	Janki Kutir	107
10.	Shabana and Baba	112
11.	He was an Unusual Man	129
	Epilogue	157
	Glossary	159

Acknowledgments

When I look back at life's highs and lows it is with a sense of wonder as well as a feeling of fulfilment. I have often thought of writing about those past times. But for long it remained just a thought. Then one day I finally mustered enough courage to put pen to paper.

My childhood was spent in Hyderabad with its vibrant culture, and its beautiful colours with mellifluous Urdu names. But the most important colour in my life was that of Kaifi whose presence fills the pages of this book. I lived an eventful, rich life with Kaifi so that, when it came to writing about it, I did not have to resort to any embellishments. I simply wrote about the past as I had lived it.

The first person I want to thank is my son-in-law, Javed Akhtar. After Kaifi passed away I lost all interest in most things, and pushed the half-finished manuscript of this book aside. It was Javed who encouraged me and persuaded me to take it up again and to complete it. And the writing helped me return to life. My daughter Shabana is like the captain who steers her ship skilfully to its destination. If Shabana had not taken it upon herself to ensure its publication, the manuscript would have been gathering dust on my bedside table.

I am not quite sure how to thank Nasreen Rehman – or Cheanie, as she is also called. Not only has Cheanie captured my voice in her beautiful translation, she suggested that the late Dr Ralph Russell write the Introduction and the scholar, Dr Priyamavada Gopal add a Foreword. I am very grateful that they have added the weight of their scholarship to my book. It was Cheanie who drew my memoir to the attention of Professor Amartya Sen, who took the trouble to make time to read it in what is by all standards a gruelling schedule. I am touched by his words of appreciation.

It gives me great pleasure that Zubaan Publishers, the hallmark of feminist writing in India, are publishing my book in English, thus taking it to a wider international audience.

Jan 2010   SHAUKAT KAIFI
Mumbai.

Introduction

❄❄

I first read this book in the Urdu original. It is a very remarkable book, made all the more so for reasons which I should perhaps begin by declaring. Shaukat Azmi is the widow of Kaifi Azmi whom I knew of, and may have met, during my first year's study leave in India in 1949–50. I knew that he was a leading Urdu poet in the Progressive Writers' Association, and in addition there was the attraction that we were both members of our respective communist parties, and very dedicated members at that. Shaukat writes of him 'He always carried his Party card in his briefcase and would often take it out and say proudly "This is my most valuable capital".' I last met him in the late 90s in Lucknow where we were both participants on a seminar on Faiz. I asked him then whether he was still a party member. He said, 'Yes, card-carrying.'

I think it relevant to say all this because, obviously, he looms large in this book. Until after his death I never knew that he was married and that Shabana Azmi, the famous film star, was his daughter. Even then I did not know anything about his wife until I received this book.

I began reading it at once, and it held my interest to the end. Its most striking quality is a sort of naivety, a naivety of a very positive and admirable kind. It seems that Shaukat has never been a communist party member, but to me this doesn't matter, because

I realized more than 50 years ago that (obviously) not every good person is a communist and (much more important) that not every communist is a good person. It's the good people who are to be valued and Shaukat is emphatically one of these. Like Kaifi, she has had a lifelong commitment to a sincere and honest life in which she exploited no-one and worked constantly for the well-being of the common people and against those who oppress and exploit them. For her, this is what politics is all about. In her long and active life she has known scores, if not hundreds, of well known left-wingers, but she makes no 'party political' (so to speak) judgements of any of them, because it is their personal qualities and the way they relate to her that concerns her. For instance, of the terrible days of Ranadive's domination of the communist party (1947-1950) she expresses no opinion of the political line, but speaks of the way in which in that period everyone came to suspect everyone else, and of the distress this caused her. Incidentally, the book gives a vivid picture of communist party life before Ranadive's advent to power, a way of life which I myself witnessed at close quarters when I was in India both in 1943–5 and in 1949–50.

An early part of the book gives a vivid picture of her girlhood and youth in Hyderabad (in Andhra Pradesh) and goes on to describe how she fell in love, virtually at first sight, with Kaifi and he with her. No other book that I know of has done anything like this, and the picture is a fascinating one, in which one sees the mingling of traditional, conventional social Muslim values with the intense romanticism, which these produce in those who break with them. Thus, before Kaifi ever declares his love for her, he responds to her speaking of a marriage that has been arranged for him by telling her 'I will never marry', without adding the unspoken words 'anyone but you'. And she tells us how soon after this she wrote to him, 'I love you, Kaifi, I love you boundlessly. No power in the world can stop me coming to you—no mountain, no river, no sea, no people, no sky, no angel, no God'—adding, with a touch of humour 'and God knows what else.' Later, when, not knowing that her letters to him had been intercepted by her family, he feels that she is no longer writing to him and no longer loves him, he cuts his wrist and writes her a letter in his blood. Their marriage caused a breach between her father and her mother. Her mother, as a believer in traditional values, never expresses in words her strong disapproval of her husband's support for their daughter, but doesn't speak to him for a whole month.

To those who do not know that supremely popular genre of Urdu poetry—the ghazal, the extravagant romanticism of this story may seem a bit over the top. To those who do know the ghazal it presents a wonderful picture of the love which the ghazal portrays, brought fully to life, so speak, with all the main ghazal characters identified and introduced to the reader—the lovers, their sympathizers, and the stern upholders of convention (in this case in Shaukat's own family) who do all they can to thwart the lovers.

Kaifi and Shaukat are both communists—that she is not a party member is not significant—and live their lives in accordance with communist principles as they understand them. Shaukat writes 'Kaifi was not only my husband, he was my friend who never imposed his own wishes on me and never made me do anything I didn't want to do. He always respected my wishes and my desires. He always tried to help me to go forward, achieve fame, be independent, and win people's praise.' Kaifi is not an actor, but Shaukat is and has a long career both on stage and in films from 1944 to 1988, and Kaifi is fully involved and fully supportive of her. Occasional disagreements are not concealed, and are resolved by happy compromise. Thus, when after many years they acquire a house of their own they discuss how it is to be furnished. Shaukat thought Kaifi's suggestions were absurd and, she writes, 'He thought mine were. Kaifi was a keen gardener, and we agreed that he should do what he liked with the garden and I should do what I liked with the house.'

Sometimes they seem to have been guided, perhaps quite unconsciously, by more traditional values. Thus, Shaukat is not a conventionally religious person, but she believes in the power of prayer. In 1973, when Kaifi suffered an attack (which eventually left his left arm paralysed) and his life was in danger she says , 'Of all his many friends, Muslim, Hindu and Sikh, there was not one who did not go to his mosque or temple or gurdwara to pray for him, and it was the effect of their prayers that he gradually recovered consciousness.' And much later on in the story, when Kaifi decides that they should leave Bombay and spend the rest of their lives in Mijwan, the extremely backward village in which Kaifi had spent his boyhood and youth, one wonders whether it is only their great mutual love which determines what they do. She says of this decision, 'The object of his life was to change the world, to banish poverty, hunger and ignorance. But when he saw that to change the whole world would take a very long time, he turned to his village. And there, he did indeed achieve a huge transformation.' Anyway, the husband decides and the wife accepts. Shaukat merely comments, 'I was living very comfortably in Bombay. Besides, I had always been a town dweller and the thought of living in a village filled me with dismay. But I knew that Kaifi would never change his mind. What could I do?' So that was that. She did live in Mijwan and worked shoulder to shoulder with Kaifi to achieve improvements in village life which in quality and quantity seem almost miraculous. And in all this their unflagging efforts were paralleled by an equally unwavering patience. She clearly concurs with Kaifi's words to her daughter, 'When you are working for change you must accept that the change may not come in your lifetime, but even so you must keep working for it.'

Shaukat's behaviour towards her two children is also determined both by her traditional and modern values.

There is much else in this book. I had not known that, like her daughter after her, she too had been a famous actress, and those more knowledgeable than I am about these things will find here the full list of the plays and films in which she has performed.

When I first read the book I learnt from the foreword that Nasreen Rehman had translated it into English, but I had not seen the translation. Now I have. It is an excellent translation, and I am very happy to have had the opportunity, at the translator's own request, to sit with her and help her finalize it. Here it is, making Shaukat's story available to a much larger audience than the Urdu original could reach.

Foreword

PRIYAMVADA GOPAL

᠅

A s I write this, arguments rage in Britain on the issue of the 'veil'—whether Muslim women living here should or should not don the full 'niqab' (which covers the face almost entirely), whether such apparel denotes patriarchal oppression or feminist assertion, whether it constitutes simple cultural assertion or an untenable rejection of integration into a multicultural society and so on. Even as the occasional Muslim woman is brought out by the media to express an opinion, the debate has been both reductive and blithely ignorant of past debate on the issue. Not only have commentators on both sides largely neglected the long and varied sociopolitical history of veiling, they have shown little awareness of the equally long and diverse history, in South Asia and elsewhere, of Muslim women speaking and writing about their lives and experiences, often alluding to practices of veiling and seclusion.

The Indian subcontinent, of course, has long been home to a vibrant tradition of women's writing which addresses not only such practices, but also a range of issues which affected women—from different communities— both in the domestic and public spheres. By the end of the 19th century, the education of women was spreading across both Hindu and Muslim communities; a host of periodicals and women's magazines like the *Indian Ladies Magazine* (English), *Stree Darpan* (Hindi) and *Mohamaddi* (Bengali) and provided forums for emerging women writers and for the discussion of issues relating to women. Urdu-speaking, predominantly Muslim communities like those based in Lucknow and Aligarh were particularly prolific in this regard with periodicals such as *Tehzib-e-Niswan* (Women's Education), *Ismat* (Virtue) and Khatoon (Woman) enjoying wide circulation. This stimulating intellectual context enabled Muslim women like Sughra Humayun Mirza, Rokeya Sakhawat Hossain and Nazar Sajjad Hyder to write fiction as well as thoughtful tracts on social issues such as the education of women and purdah (or seclusion).[1]

As the mid-twentieth century approached, Muslim women from upper- and middle-class homes were not only heavily involved in social reform activities in their own communities but also engaged with nationalist and, very often, with socialist politics. Writers such as Rashid Jahan, Ismat Chughtai, and Razia Sajjad Zaheer had independent careers as teachers, screenwriters and doctors in addition to which they took part in political activism. The decades leading up to and following Independence in 1947 were, of course, a time of literary and cultural ferment as the Progressive Writers Association (founded in 1936) and the Indian People's Theatre Association (est. 1942) made their impact felt across the country. These organizations included both socialists and fellow-travellers who all 'shared the conviction that art, literature and film cold help shape and transform the nascent nation state in progressive directions'.[2] Many of India's most well-known Urdu writers—Sajjad Zaheer, Kishen Chander, Rajinder Singh Bedi, Saadat Hasan Manto and Khwaja Ahmad Abbas—emerged from within the Progressive ambit. Although like many other political and cultural organizations, these groups were often male-dominated, there is no doubt that the PWA and IPTA provided a space in which many women did come into their own as writers, performers and

---

[1] See Susie Tharu and K. Lalita (eds) (1993 and 1994), *Women Writing in India: 600 BC to the Present Day*, New York: The Feminist Press; Eunice de Souza (ed.), *Purdah*, New Delhi: Oxford University Press, 1995.

[2] Gopal, Priyamvada (2006), *Literary Radicalism in India: Gender, Nation and the Transition to Independence*, Oxford, Routledge.

artistes. Women, particularly Urdu-speaking women from Muslim communities, like Rashid Jahan, Razia Sajjad Zaheer, Ismat Chughtai, Hajrah Begum and Zohra Sehgal, found distinctive ways of articulating their voices within these institutions even as they—inevitably—had to negotiate left-wing patriarchy and its own brand of gender politics.

Shaukat Kaifi's autobiography emerges in part out of this heady milieu and is peopled by many of the women mentioned above as well as other luminaries from Progressive circles. Born to a progressive upper-class family in the princely state of Hyderabad, Shaukat would find herself attending mushairas (poetry recitals) and literary discussions where she came into contact with the radical young poets and writers such as Sardar Jafri and Majrooh Sultanpuri, who would form the backbone of the Progressive movements. It is at one such event that she meets and falls in love with the dashing young poet, Kaifi Azmi, whom she would marry against the wishes of her mother and extended family. The account of their breathless and unconventional courtship is one of the most lively sections of her autobiography, complete with elaborate flirtation, yearning love poetry, clandestine letters (one written in blood), broken engagements, parental obstruction, suicide threats and a near elopement. This part of her account shows something of the influence of the 'afsana' tradition in Urdu literature; like many other women writers of her time, she would have read something of these romantic stories even as later life would have brought the leavening influence of realism. But there is nothing passive or wilting about the young Shaukat as recalled by her older self: the young woman we meet is flirtatious, assertive and charmingly aware of her own striking attributes. Commanded by a newly-pious brother to don a burqa, she recalls that since nobody in the older generation wore this piece of apparel, the family did not even own one she and her sister could press into service which she, in any case, would refuse to do. Instead she delights in the distinctly secular joys of 'dyeing and crinkling' colourful dupattas, exquisite kargaa cloth, Hyderabadi bangles and saris with intricate zari kamdani or brocade work.

Marriage to Kaifi entailed all kinds of transitions—from the relatively sheltered environs of princely Hyderabad to the rough commercial bustle of Bombay, and from the 'fairytale-like atmosphere' of the ancestral home to a commune where the 'frugal disarray' of a small room throws down a challenge to Shaukat's formidable domestic skills. Throughout her narrative, Shaukat lovingly details her passion for domesticity and beauty—her passion for elaborate Hyderabadi cooking, exquisite textiles and carefully-chosen furnishings—even against the grain of straitened circumstances. As the wife of a 'whole-timer' and poet who 'spent most in his time in worker's area [lying] with them on a shaggy charpoy and—and [writing] poetry, it was she who had to pay attention to the humdrum details of daily life in the 'Movement'. This is a valuable text not least for its account of daily life in a CPI commune from the gendered perspective of a wife and mother. Told by the famed party leader, P.C. Joshi, that the 'wife of a Communist' must not sit idle, Shaukat finds work as a radio artiste, launching her long, illustrious and independent career as an actor. The prose of this memoir is imbued with a markedly dramatic sensibility as is evident from the several sections where Shaukat moves away from direct narration to recounting episodes in the form of short theatrical interludes. Though self-conscious about unlearning her 'bourgeois Hyderabadi lifestyle', Shaukat is also able to bring the critical perspective of an outsider to what she sees around her. If she asserts that the Party is 'a large family where everyone loved and cared for one another', she is also able to recall that at the Progressive Writers Conference her grief at the death of her infant son, Khayyam, makes 'people uncomfortable…and walk away'. In a more troubling claim, she speaks of her determination to keep her second pregnancy though the 'orders' are 'given for her to have an abortion'.

As many feminist scholars have shown, autobiographies form a particularly rich seam in the landscape of women's writing in India. Memoirs by women involved with the theatre and related artistic forms constitute a particularly interesting sub-genre. As accounts by

the legendary Bengali actor, Binodini Dasi, and the Marathi, Hamsa
Wadkar (on which the award-winning film *Bhumika* is based) suggest,
these were women who were among the first to negotiate the shifting
boundaries of public and private as the 19th century brought with
it changes in family and social structures and mores.[3] Their status
as 'public' women served to define the middle-class housewife as
respectable in her 'private' domain. Binodini and Hansa's memoirs
are filled with an ambiguous yearning to become what they would
never really be allowed to be—wives and mothers—even as they
clearly also relish the double-edged freedoms that define their lives
as well as what they are able to accomplish as working women.
Shaukat's memoir, in contrast, is conscious of the transitional status
of the actress in a postcolonial era in an India proud of its officially
egalitarian modernity. As she sets off for work at the Prithvi theatres
with the baby Shabana strapped to her back, she is both proud of
being able to contribute to the family wage and prickly about the
ambiguous social implications of her new profession, identifying
as she does with 'respectable' middle-class women whom she then
addresses: 'Whatever you do in your homes I too can do that, but
can you stand on stage and deliver long dialogue? I can, therefore I
am superior to you'.

Something of a desire to fill in the historical gaps also animates
Shaukat's account; she remarks quite rightly on the paucity of
materials on IPTA and Prithvi theatres, formative institutions in
the history of Indian theatre: 'This is a weakness I have noticed
in us artists; we do not know how to document our art'. We get
tantalizing glimpses of the hustle and bustle of political theatre
as writers like Ismat Chughtai and K.A. Abbas spin out plays on
activist themes and young actors who would eventually become
famous—like Zohra Sehgal, Sanjeev Kumar and Shaukat herself—
cut their teeth with mass audiences. Though occasionally devolving
into a hagiographic mode when it comes to Prithviraj Kapoor, the
larger-than-life founder of Prithvi Theatres and the patriarch of

[3] *Amar Katha* and *Sangate Aika*.

the famous theatre-and-film clan which still dominates the Bombay film industry, Shaukat's account of working with this group gives us insights into the daily life of a theatre company seeking to establish itself both as a medium of entertainment and a consciousness-raising endeavour. We hear of voice-training sessions which involve singing multi-faith prayers, Kapoor's espousal of the Stanislawski method, the rejection of the 'Parsi theatre' way of doing this and tours across India where Shaukat herself sees and learns much.[4] The brief but tantalizing section on IPTA recalls the ferment of an active theatrical movement, many of whose plays and dramatizations are now lost to historical record. Shaukat, like many others involved with Prithvi and IPTA, then makes the transition to films, becoming a well-known character actor in films like *Heer-Ranjha*, *Umrao Jaan*, *Bazaar*, *Garm Hawa* and *Salaam Bombay*.

Kaifi and I is also a story of family life in unusual and changing circumstances. Since neither parent holds down a steady, salaried job, economic uncertainty becomes fact of life even as both children, Shabana and Baba, are somehow given the best possible education and opportunities. As success comes to Kaifi's career as a lyricist and Shaukat finds acting opportunities, things frequently improve. Like many Muslim families, this one too is inevitably affected by Partition and the migration of close relatives to newly-formed Pakistan. Animated by Shaukat and Kaifi's enormous love and her profound and continuing sense of loss after his death, this memoir is also the portrait of a modern marriage with its own joys, compromises, crises and triumphs. Though she takes enormous pride in his achievements as poet and writer, exasperation at Kaifi's careless bohemian ways when it comes to financial and household matters erupts through Shaukat's reminiscences. Suffused also with maternal pride, Shaukat's memories of raising her gifted children who would become well-known in their own right are carefully articulated. Even so the narrative conveys the obviously strong bond between mother and daughter, the actor and activist, Shabana Azmi, forged in the crucible the minor conflicts and differences that temper all filial relationships.

Peppered throughout with his poetry, *Kaifi and I* is ultimately unimaginable without Kaifi's huge literary, intellectual and emotional presence even as it paints in vivid brushstrokes, the portrait of a woman who is very much her own person as wife, mother and creative force. The account of his illness and the years leading up to his death are harrowing and testify, arguably, to the ways in which this is very much a gendered narrative where the domestic and public are not separable in any easy way and where the personal and the professional inflect each other in complex ways. The grief-filled voice that breaks through in the final paragraphs ignores the reader and addresses itself to Kaifi directly, in the personal and performative mode of 'biraha', the lament of the unconsoled beloved, 'How long will I have to go on living without you?' This is a voice that is strong and distinctive in its own right, but with a timbre enriched by beloved, family and comrades. The memoir of an individual, it reminds us, is also inevitably the story of the many. What you have before you is one such chronicle of the elusive past and evanescent present.

Translator's Note

Nasreen Rehman

I have long admired Shaukat Kaifi Sahiba's work as an actor and for decades have enjoyed her hospitality in Janki Kutir, Bombay and the village Mijwan. It was during the winter of 2001 at Kaifi Sahib's birthday celebration that I first heard her read from her engaging memoir, a work in progress at the time. Her beloved Kaifi died in May 2002 and she finished the book as a testament of love; *Yaad ki Rehguzar* (Memory Lane) was published in 2004. When the author asked me to translate the book into English, I was delighted but also nervous at the possibility of her turning around and saying, in her singular manner, 'I appreciate all the hard work you have put in, but I am sorry, I cannot accept this; it is not my voice.' I am relieved that my translation has her approval.

Kaifi and I is a love story, but it is also an important corrective to the proliferating stereotypical representations of Muslims as conservative moderns, incapable of engaging with liberal and progressive politics or secular concerns. The book is a montage of recollections moving between the city and the village, interspersed with poetry, reportage of direct speech, theatre pieces and snippets of screenplays, bringing into focus an autochthonous modernity rooted in middle-class Muslim and Urdu speaking milieus. Shaukat Kaifi Sahiba's life is lived at an intersection where communist, progressive, and nationalist politics converge with literature, cinema, popular culture and everyday life. (See Introduction and Foreword)

In translating this book I have tried to capture the tenor of the author's prose, which has the spontaneity of conversation, and is never florid. I have retained Urdu words where I thought this was the best way of conveying the author's intentions. The use of honorifics like Sahiba (Madam) and kinship terms such as Mamun (maternal uncle) may sound odd to some readers of English, but they convey a very good sense of the South Asian emphasis on the etiquette of address and the ordering of familial relationships. The well known Urdu scholar Dr Ralph Russell asked me why I had not used 'gold thread' and 'gold embroidery' for 'gota', 'zari', 'kamdani' and 'karchob', and agreed with my usage after I had explained the differences between these various braids and embroideries. He agreed that I retain the names of flowers, food and items of clothing: a gharara, a shalwar and a churidar pyjama are trousers or pantaloons of sorts, but they are very different from each other; qaliya and qorma are both meat curries but this is where the similarity ends; and a mogra flower is not simply a jasmine. For the reader familiar with these worlds, the terms will evoke a picture very close to the one that the author intended; for others, I hope that with the help of the glossary (Appendix 1) her world will become more vivid. In translating the poetry, after long discussions with Russell Sahib, I decided not to recreate the poems but render into simple English poetry that is in fairly complex Urdu, in order to give the reader some flavour of the original.

Readers who are familiar with *Yaad Ki Rehguzar* in Urdu will find some additions in this book; these have not been inserted arbitrarily by me. My publisher Urvashi Butalia and I had questions where we wanted the author to expand upon her feelings about certain matters or clarify an ambiguity. I spent several weeks with Shaukat Kaifi Sahiba, reading the first draft of the translation to her and discussing our queries. She was forthright in responding to my questions, but firm in insisting exactly how and where she wanted these additions. I took some editorial liberties, particularly in restoring the end of the book in accordance with the author's first Urdu draft: again, I had her permission to do so.

There are people I would like to thank for giving generously of their time to read and comment on the various drafts of my translation: Shabana Azmi for her crucial editorial input; Shaheen Choudhury, Antonia Douro, Mariam Faruqi, Nasheed Faruqi and Katy Fizmon for important stylistic suggestions; and Urvashi Butalia for her patience. My debt is greatest to two individuals who are not here to see this book in print, my mother Begum Qamar F.R. Khan (d. 6th March 2008) and Dr Ralph Russell (d. 13th September 2008). Amma who had loved the book in Urdu was involved enthusiastically in the process of translation. I had four day-long sittings with Russell Sahib who was generous in the spirit of the ustad shagird relationship. His praise was warm, his criticism acute, but softened by his hospitality as he fed me lunch, tea and cakes through a strictly timed routine. In Delhi, the late Dr Bharat Ram and his family, provided me a home during long and frequent visits. Finally, I would like to thank Shaukat Kaifi Sahiba for trusting me with her book. I am mindful of the responsibility, and hope I have been able to capture for the reader something of the flavour of the original.

1

Growing up in Hyderabad

I was born into a family that was mildly progressive. My father
Yahya Khan was a champion of girls' education but his father
Hakim Inayatullah Khan and brother Ayub Ali Khan were decidedly
against it. Abbajan wanted my older sisters Liaqat Khanam and Riasat
Khanam to have the best available education and enrolled them in
the local mission school in the face of strong opposition from his
entire family. The school was co-educational, which meant that the
question of purdah had to be tackled; on this matter too, Abbajan's
position was equally clear: as early as 1907 he had persuaded Ammajan
to relinquish purdah. Soon after they were married and were on their
way to Hyderabad from their ancestral village of Saharanpur Lohari
in north India, Ammajan packed away her burqah in an attaché case
at Delhi railway station.

Hyderabad, which was the largest and most prosperous princely
state in India, was ruled by the Nizam who was perhaps the richest
man in the world at the time. Young men from all over India went
there in search of employment. One such, Latif Yar Jang, had
moved to Hyderabad from Lohari in the late nineteenth century.
He secured a comfortable position in the State administration and
did everything in his power to promote talented young men from
his village. It was through his good offices that men from Abbajan's
family moved to Hyderabad to complete their education and find

suitable employment. Latif Yar Jang was distantly related to us and the children of our family called him Latif Dada. My real Dada was an orthodox maulvi and a scholar of Arabic and Persian who had translated the Holy Qur'an into Urdu. He ensured that my father completed his classical Arabic and Persian education but excluded instruction in English as he was against everything British. However, when it became clear to Abbajan that without English he would not get a good job, he decided to study it on the quiet and passed his matriculation. Such was my father's command over the language that he could teach B.A. students.

Throughout his life Abbajan enjoyed teaching and spent a great deal of his leisure time tutoring children. When he got a job as an Inspector in the Excise Department Abbajan had to study Telugu, as this was mandatory for official employment in Hyderabad. Abbajan had regular features with exceptionally kind, light brown eyes and he looked taller than his five foot ten inches. My mother Khatoon Khanam was a good-looking Pathan with a fair oval face and large black eyes. They made a handsome couple. Ammajan was a good and prudent wife who followed her husband's bidding but with dignity. Although she was unable to read or write Ammajan respected learning. Both my parents observed the Islamic strictures on fasting and prayed five times a day. There was no pressure on me to do so, but like all other members of my family, I too offered my prayers. Ever curious to learn, I would read the Holy Qur'an in its Urdu translation because I wanted to find out for myself what was so special about the holy book that half the world had faith in it. My sister, Riasat Khanam, had finished reading the Holy Qur'an in Arabic when she was seven and before she was nine, had committed the entire book to memory and become a hafiz.

In my parents' generation it was not uncommon for couples to have many children and they had twelve, of whom ten survived infancy. Their firstborn was my sister Liaqat Khanam who was called Bari Apajan by all her younger siblings; Riasat Khanam or Choti Apajan followed her. Next was our brother Zakaria, who died when he was eighteen months old. The fourth was Bare Bhaijan, Khurshid Ali Khan; and the fifth was Chote Bhaijan Naimatullah Khan. Two years after him on 20 October 1928, I arrived as the sixth child. Another sister, Sardar Khanam followed me, but she died of heart trouble when she was eighteen years old. The next in line was my brother Nasrullah Khan, whom we called Nawabjani; and after him another sister called Sadat Khanam who died when she was twenty days old. Finally, there were my three younger sisters, Qamar Khanam, Zafar Khanam and Iqbal Khanam. My younger siblings called me Apa Bi, while older members of the family called me Moti, because they thought my teeth were like pearls.

In 1941, when I was thirteen years old and in class six at school, Abbajan's monthly salary was three hundred rupees, which was sufficient for him to educate his children and look after the household. Bare Bhaijan was studying for his B.A. at Osmania University where he lived in the hostel; his monthly expenditure was twenty-one rupees. My sisters' tutor, a Telugu Christian called Mallapa, was paid fifteen rupees a month. He arrived at five o'clock in the morning and was served breakfast, which in our home was simple khichri, chutney, yoghurt, and papadums, and as an occasional treat, qeema. The lady cook, or the mama, earned eight rupees a month. The task of bringing the month's supply of dry rations, which included ghee and firewood for cooking, was delegated to Bare Bhaijan and he managed this on forty rupees.

My sisters and I went to school in a shikram, a cart drawn by two bullocks, in which we would sit facing each other in an enclosure that was curtained off on all sides. Often, driving through a bazaar called Mangal Haat we would hear the voice of the legendary Begum Akhtar singing Behzad Lucknavi's ghazal *Divana banana hai to divana bana de* (Intoxicate me if you wish), competing with cries from a butcher's shop, 'Buy a quarter seer for just four gande!' As a princely state, Hyderabad had its own currency called Hali in which a ganda was four paisas and six paisas made an anna. One rupee was made of solid silver and had ninety-six paisas. The parts of India that were ruled by the British used the Kaldar currency, with four paisas to an anna and sixteen annas to a rupee. In Hyderabad the months too, had different names, for example, Azur, Dei, Bahman, Isfander, Ferverdi, Ardi Behisht, Khurdad, Teer, Amardad, Shehrevar, Mehr and Aban, according to the Persian lunar calendar. Colours too, were called by beautiful Urdu names such as *zafrani*(saffron yellow), *kasni*(light purple), *pyazi*(pink), *katthae*(brown), *uda*(purple), *turai ke phool ka rang*(yellow), *sabz*(green), *motia rang*(pearly pink), *asmani*(light blue), *surmai*(grey), *shaftalu*(maroon), *kahi*(bottle green) *unabi*(maroon), *lal*(red), *morkanthi ka rang*(turquoise), *baingani*(purple), *sandali*(beige) – and many more that I cannot recall. When I was a schoolgirl, these words were standard Urdu usage. It is a pity that over time they have been lost to English.

I was an expert at dyeing and crinkling my dupattas and could make any colour by blending two, three colours or more. It gave me endless pleasure to match my dupattas with my kurtas. Ammajan recognized my talent and supplied me with a worktable, boxes of colours, brushes, glue and all the paraphernalia that I required. I used plain muslin, which cost two annas a yard and, with that, I could create a gorgeous dupatta for four or five annas. I would spend a great deal of time in planning my wardrobe and enjoyed flaunting it at school. It was not unusual for girls to peep into my classroom to admire my latest creation.

I have always had an eye for textiles and enjoyed nothing more than accompanying my mother and older sisters on their shopping sprees. My older sisters wore muslin saris to school, and could buy these for anything between two and a half to six rupees each. Unbelievable as it may sound today, but in my childhood it was possible to buy the most exquisite French chiffon sari for ten rupees. When Bari Apajan got married in 1939, if I recall correctly, gold was forty rupees a tola, while a sari with real gold zari kamdani or karchob work was thirty to forty rupees. A particular favourite of mine was karga, an exquisite white cotton net finely embroidered in white counted threadwork, which at eighteen rupees a yard, was expensive. For weddings and other special occasions such as Eid, young girls wore karga kurtas with the intricately draped, six-yard long khara dupattas while older women wore shorter karga kurtas with their saris. Essential for all girls and coveted throughout India, were joray, the Hyderabadi bangles set with artificial stones, which were imported from Germany and sparkled like precious gems. Although joray are made to this day it is no longer possible to find the same dazzling colours.

There were other aspects of Hyderabadi culture that were rather appealing. Young girls would keep jasmine flowers and sweet-scented kevra leaves between the folds of their clothes. They would steam their freshly washed hair by spreading it over a basket containing an earthenware pot full of embers and agar; the fragrance would remain in the hair for days. These attractive baskets were an indispensable part of a girl's dowry. Surrounded by the fragrance of kevra, khas and agar, and radiant in their colourful khara dupattas, Hyderabadi girls were like creatures from a fairytale world – and I delighted in being one of them.

Hyderabadis took great pride in their food. The cuisine was a blend of the United Provinces and South Indian kitchens, and this fusion of north and south made it distinct. Everyday fare on a table like ours included favourites like bagharay baingan, mirchon ka khatta salan, tamatar ka kat, gosht ki karhi, mahi qaliya. For special feasts there were delicacies like biryani, qorma, dam ke kebab, luqmia and tatti ke kebab. The word tatti does not sound very pleasing because of its scatological association but in this instance it simply means a mat of steel put on flaming coals. Eaten straight off the metal grills the kebab are deliciously succulent.

Ammajan, who ran a first rate kitchen, was assiduous in helping the poor and she did so without making a fuss. Every Thursday, an ill-tempered old crone would turn up for lunch. All of us found her presence irksome but my sister Sardar Khanam was particularly peeved by this old hag who would sit outside her window, chomping away noisily. Sardar would demand in typical Hyderabadi, 'Hey lady, why d'ya come here?' and the old woman would respond in equally broad Hyderabadi, 'Hey, I'm here 'cause I'm fed!' Another regular was an old woman whose style of begging was quite unique. She carried a wooden doll with hands made of painted tin. Hiding her own hands under the doll's clothes, she would clap the tin hands and sing along to the percussion in Hyderabadi.

Where did the money go, Ma?
The money should not have gone
If I had the money I would get some hemru
The husband would have a shervani
The wife would have a choli
The child would have a hat
The servant girl would have a bag
O, where did the money go, Ma?

If I had the money I would get some meat
The husband would eat biryani
The wife would eat qorma
The child would eat bone marrow
The dog would eat a bone
How did the money go, Ma?
That money had to go.

I had six friends, Amina, Shamim, Atiya, Mohsina, Mehdi and Dilshad. I was particularly fond of Amina, because not only was she quite gorgeous, she was also amiable, well turned out and carried the familiar fragrance of flowers and agar. Our friendship developed during the rehearsal of our annual school play, *Adl-e-Jahangir* (Jahangir's Justice). I played the role of the Mughal Emperor Jahangir and Amina that of his consort Noor Jahan. Dressed in her finery Amina could easily have passed off as the Empress. A few months ago I was deeply grieved to learn that my dear Amina had died in Pakistan. I had met her in Karachi not much earlier, and even though she was suffering from heart disease her spirit had not been dimmed. She was stylishly turned out and her large eyes were as lustrous as ever. My friend Atiya Shahnawaz, a bright-eyed girl with a flawless complexion and a fine figure, was the village belle in our school play. Atiya has looked after herself and remains as attractive as a grandmother as she was when we were at school. Shamim, whose family had come to Hyderabad from Azamgarh, was tall and slim with a dusky complexion. Today she lives in Chicago with her daughter Anjum. Shamim too has not changed very much, I am the only one who has put on so much weight. I lost touch with Mohsina, Mehdi and Dilshad after I got married. Perhaps, their families moved away to Pakistan at Partition.

In Hyderabad, the comfortable world of the wealthy and the middle classes stood out in stark contrast against the wretched condition of the poor. Often during our school holidays we would go with Abbajan on his tours around the State and stay in various dak bungalows. I saw that, as a matter of course, Abbajan's peons were brutal to the dhair, the local low-caste, who would be dragged from their homes and forced to work for us. If we happened to be staying in a very small place where there was no dak bungalow, the dhair would pitch our tents, fetch water from the well, dust and clean our living quarters and perform any other tasks expected of them.

Abbajan was not in the habit of making demands on the poor, but this was not the case with both my maternal uncles who were sub-inspectors in the excise department. They would requisition chicken, ghee and whatever else they wanted from these unfortunate people. My uncles had no qualms about using force: the dhair who dared to disobey them was thrashed cruelly. An old man who refused to work was forced to stand through the night with a stone slab tied to his back. I was horrified and lay awake the whole night thinking of the poor helpless man. Perhaps, the beginnings of the Telangana Movement were in response to such oppression. I do not think that anybody in Andhra would put up with such cruelty today.

In the feudal society of Hyderabad, even the gentry did not feel entirely secure. If Nizam Sarkar, who was also called A'la Hazrat, was expected at a wedding, all girls aged between fourteen and twenty-four were hidden away for fear of Sarkar's gaze. If a girl took the Nizam's fancy she was forced to enter his harem. Worse than their ruler were the licentious men from some of the Yar Jung families, who were a part of the Hyderabadi elite. At school, I would hear countless stories about these depraved Jung boys. A young girl whom they had abducted from the roadside, died after she had been tied to a tamarind tree and gang-raped. The punishment prescribed by Nizam Sarkar for the young men guilty of this barbarous act was that their fathers had to wear shackles made of flowers: what mockery of the girl's suffering!

I recall an evening soon after Bari Apajan's wedding, when Chote Bhaijan and I were returning with her from her friend Shah Jahan's house in an open tonga. We decided to call on our family friend, Doctor Abu'l Fazal Sahib, a homeopath who lived near Sagar Talkies cinema. By the time we reached his house it was dusk. Chote Bhaijan went inside to enquire after Doctor Sahib while Apajan and I waited in the tonga. Apajan was looking exquisite in her finery. We had not been there long when a car drove up and stopped near us. A man wearing a dark shervani got out, walked up to us and addressed Bari Apajan most courteously. 'Please, come with me.'

'Where?' asked Apajan.

'Sahib is calling you,' answered the man as I felt a shiver run down my spine. Grabbing Bari Apajan's hand, I said, 'Run, they are Jung boys!' Such was the notoriety of these boys that the tonga-wallah sat silently through this exchange, as though oblivious to what was happening. We jumped out of the tonga and fled, with the car following us. We were almost run over as it screeched to a halt barely two feet away from us. Breathless, we rushed into Doctor Sahib's dispensary. Chote Bhaijan who was a fearless Pathan, was enraged by the affront to his sisters' honour and though barely sixteen at the time, he rushed out, stuck his head into the car and roared, 'Who dared to ask, "Come with me?" Are you not ashamed of stalking the wives and daughters of respectable families?'

'Oh no, Sir,' one of them answered with affectation, 'we saw these ladies running across the road and simply wanted to help. We were worried lest they be run over by a car.' We did not want the men to find out where we lived, so instead of going home we headed off in the opposite direction to a friend's house in Malak Peth. The car followed us all the way there and then drove off.

When His Eminence the Nizam ventured forth and his motorcade progressed through the streets of Hyderabad it was obligatory for everyone to stand to attention. Cars, rickshaws, cycles, passersby, everyone and everything had to come to a halt. All the children in my family had been warned, that if ever we were in the vicinity of the royal motorcade, we were to lower our eyes and stand still or we would be struck blind. Even I, who was fearless in most matters, complied with these orders. I recall a particularly tragic incident involving a young man who had to cross a road on his motorbike, just as His Eminence was due to drive past. Perhaps, it was because he thought nobody would notice him that the young man ignored the police whistles and crossed the road, speeding into an alleyway, just as the Nizam's motorcade drove by. The Begum Sahiba spotted him and ordered her car to stop. The young man was hauled up; the fact that he was from an eminent Jung family was not enough to save him from humiliation. All the children on the street were ordered to spit on him. Unable to bear this insult he killed himself. The following morning his body was found in the Gandi Peth pond. I recoiled from the cruel injustice of what had happened, although I suspect that, for most other members of my family, the young man's tragedy was a part of everyday life.

The Nizam was an archetypal prince who could be cruel or refined at will. He was a prominent patron of the arts in general and in particular of Urdu, which was the official language of the state and compulsory in every school. He founded the Osmania University where all instruction was in Urdu. Many scholars regard Hyderabad as the birthplace of Urdu and base their claim on the culture that produced the poetry of the king, Mohammad Quli Qutb Shah and

the poet, Wali Dakkani. In my childhood Urdu was alive and well
in Hyderabad and many newspapers, journals and periodicals were
published from here in the language.

༺༻

In due course, Abbajan was promoted and posted to Aurangabad as
an Excise Superintendent. He had the use of a splendid house, a car,
a telephone and twelve household staff. Aurangabad was a big city
with good schools and colleges and Ammajan joined Abbajan there
with some of my brothers and sisters. By now Bare Bhaijan who was
married to Nafis Khanam, my Phupi's rather good looking daughter
from Lohari, was also living in Aurangabad. It was comforting for my
parents to have their eldest son in the same city, because by now both
my older sisters were married and had moved away to Warangal.

I was in class nine when I had a nasty attack of malaria and my
sisters invited me for a change of air. In Warangal I lived with Bari
Apajan who was headmistress of the local girls' high school. She
was away at work all day while I was at home on my own. Boredom
soon set in. Bari Apajan decided to keep me occupied and arranged
for me to help out at her school, teaching girls of class four and five.
I was very young but evidently, well-liked. Every morning I would
enter the classroom to find garlands of fresh flowers left on my desk
by some of my students. I was in Warangal for almost two years, and
this meant that my own schooling was interrupted. However, when I
returned to my parents in Aurangabad I joined my matric class.

Choti Apajan was married to Akhtar Bhai, a Progressive writer and
poet who was invited to Hyderabad in 1946 by Qazi Abdul Ghaffar,
of *Laila ke Khutut* (Laila's Letters) fame, to join him as editor of the
Urdu daily, *Payam*. Akhtar Bhai was a gracious host and Choti Apajan
was always by his side in their open house where writers from the
Progressive Writers' Movement, such as Makhdoom Mohiuddin,
were regular visitors.

In February 1947 a Progressive Writers' Conference was organized in Hyderabad and Akhtar Bhai arranged for the poets Kaifi

Azmi and Majrooh Sultanpuri to stay with his elder sister, Baji. His younger sister Rabia Burney lived next door, and it was here that Sardar Jafri was staying with his friend Sultana, who later became his wife. Fortuitously, this was during the long school holidays, and as I happened to be visiting my sister in Hyderabad, I was able to attend the Conference and meet the Progressive Writers about whom I had heard so much. In Hyderabad it was not uncommon for writers with the slightest claim to fame to put on airs and treat with disdain those whom they considered less fortunate or famous than themselves. The young progressive writers were a refreshing change; they wore their fame so lightly that I was overwhelmed. Little did I know that this chance encounter would change my life forever.

༙

One night there was a mushaira. I was sitting in the front row with Bare Bhaijan. The air was filled with expectation. Finally, I was going to hear the celebrated poets. I had spent hours before a mirror, trying on one kurta after another and had settled on a white kargah kurta, a white shalwar, a dupatta skilfully dyed in the colours of the rainbow and golden salimshahi shoes. I was determined to overshadow all the other young women. When Kaifi began to recite his poem *Taj* (Crown), I felt impelled to fix my gaze on this tall, slim and charismatic young man, whose voice, God help me, had a timbre like the rumble of storm clouds. How brave of him to recite a powerful poem against monarchy and injustice in the Nizam's city! Bare Bhaijan turned to me and said, 'Such a bold poem from one so young; these people are truly fearless.' After the mushaira people rushed towards the three poets with their autograph books. College girls swarmed around Kaifi like flies but I preferred to wait my turn, and giving him an arch look, I turned towards Sardar Jafri and asked for his autograph instead.

After the crowds had dispersed, I walked up to Kaifi with great confidence and held out my autograph book to him. From the corner

of his eye Kaifi had caught me going towards Sardar Jafri; and to my
dismay he scribbled some meaningless couplets in my book.

> *The flaming cloud that seems to shine*
> *The earth of the nightingale's honour*
>
> *Come into my domain like a secret*
> *My heart bell rings and lightning swings*
>
> *Grab the beauty and come into my heart.*

I was miffed. Kaifi had inscribed a charming couplet for my friend
Zakia who was beaming with delight and I was consumed with envy.
When we returned to Choti Apajan's, I joined Kaifi on the steps
leading to the house and demanded petulantly, 'Why did you write
such silly couplets for me?'

'Why did you ask for Jafri Sahib's autograph first?' Kaifi asked
mischievously. He was pleased to see that I was amused in spite
of myself and we sat right there on the steps, slipping into a
conversation as though we were old friends. The eagle eyed Choti
Apajan descended upon us announcing, 'Dinner is served.' Then she
continued, 'and yes, Kaifi don't forget to congratulate Shaukat; she's
getting married in three months time to Usman, our Mamun's son.'
Kaifi's crestfallen expression mirrored my dismay, as we made our
way to dinner. I had learnt from Sardar Jafri that Kaifi was getting
married to some lady in Bombay who wanted to have a shervani
made for him, and that too of hemru, a rich brocade, which was a
specialty of our region. I could not help but feel a twinge of envy.

After dinner Kaifi and I returned to sit on the steps. 'In three
months you'll be married and you won't even think of me.' Kaifi said
in a very subdued voice.

'And you'll go back to Bombay and get married,' was my rejoinder.

'Now, I will never get married, not for the rest of my life,' Kaifi
declared.

'Marriage is a must,' I counselled him like an agony aunt, 'without
marriage life is incomplete… a human being remains unfulfilled…'

I was rambling on when I caught Kaifi staring at me. Avoiding his gaze, I rushed off to my room! Something had stirred in me – an emotion unfamiliar but exciting. I could not wait for dawn to break.

Next morning, I went into Kaifi's room. He was standing there, wearing a pair of grey trousers and a white shirt. Fresh from his bath, there were drops of water glistening on his long black hair. I had with me the perfume 'Evening in Paris' which was all the rage at the time. Purposefully, I rushed up to Kaifi and daubed some on his chest. As I turned around and ran I could sense his eyes full of laughter following me out of the room.

Kaifi went for a meeting after breakfast and disappeared for the whole day. In the evening, Akhtar Bhai and Baji were hosting a dinner party; Zakia and I were flitting around preening ourselves. It was eight o'clock and there was no sign of Kaifi. Zakia said, 'I think, Kaifi is asleep at Rabia's house.'

'Go, go and wake him up,' I urged her.

'Why should I?' she asked. I was just saying, 'Indeed, and why would I…' when Kaifi walked into the room.

I was standing by a window, near an earthenware pot of cold water, covered with an engraved silver bowl. Kaifi walked up to me and said, 'I am very thirsty.' I filled the bowl with water and offered it to him.

He said, 'More'.

I refilled the bowl. He said, 'More,'

I poured some more.

'More', said Kaifi.

I looked at him questioningly.

He said, 'My thirst is unquenched.'

Flushed, I hurried away. My world was transformed into a kaleidoscope of colours.

৩❀৩

Preparations had been made for a mushaira. There was romance in the air. The floor was covered with white sheets called chandini.

Placed here and there were silver bowls full of jasmine blossoms, which filled the air with their heady fragrance. Local poets from Hyderabad joined Majrooh, Kaifi and Sardar Jafri, making themselves comfortable against white bolsters. The proceedings began with Majrooh reciting in tarannum,

> *My destination was in sight and the wind changed direction*
> *As your hand came into my hand lamps lit up my path.*

Cries of appreciation filled the air and as Majrooh took his bow, Sardar Jafri stepped forward. Combing his fingers through his thick, long hair—a characteristic gesture, I was to learn—he tossed his head back and addressed us in his deep attractive voice, 'I am in the process of composing a long poem, in the masnavi form. It is called, 'Greetings to the New World', I shall recite the final part.'

The Caravan of Life

> *On this thoroughfare of people the caravan of life moves*
> *Bearing the heavy burden of centuries*
> *Obscuring the lustre of beautiful forms*
> *Under the dusty layers of passing time*
> *With dreams of past civilizations*
> *Asleep like hopes in a young mother's lap.*
>
> *Travellers who set out for new horizons,*
> *Carrying with them the flame of time*
> *These knights of rebellion and armies of revolution*
> *Have their feet on the ground, their sights on the sky*
> *Arise, and join these wanderers*
> *For whom time is the dust that blurs their path.*

I listened to him spellbound. I used to pride myself on being well read in contemporary Urdu literature and had enjoyed the satirical works of Shafiq-ur-Rahman and Azim Beg Chughtai; I had relished Ismat Chughtai's caustic observation of human nature and enjoyed Makhdoom's poetry; but Sardar Jafri's poem made me sit up. Clearly, these people were driven by a distinct mission in life. Irresistibly, I was drawn to Kaifi and his world, which I thought was superior to the one that I inhabited. Requests for Kaifi's poem *Aurat* (Woman) filled the air. At the time there were some standard requests at every mushaira. It was mandatory for Sahir to recite his poem *Taj Mahal* and Kaifi could not take his bow without reciting *Aurat*. I had heard rich praise for his poem and was longing to hear it. Kaifi stepped forward in complete command of the moment; he lit a cigarette, held it in his right hand, pushed back his hair with his left, and began to recite.

Woman

Arise, my love, for now you must march with me
Flames of war are ablaze in our world today
Time and fate have the same aspirations today
Our tears will flow like hot lava today
Beauty and love have one life and one soul today
You must burn in the fire of freedom with me
Arise, my love, for now you must march with me.

Patience will not help you struggle through life
Blood, not tears, sustains the pulse of life
You will fly when you're free and not ensnared by love
Heaven is not just in the arms of the man you love
Walk unfettered on the path of freedom with me
Arise, my love, for now you must march with me.

Wherever you go sacrifice awaits you
To surrender is a way of life for you
All your charms condemn you
The ways of the world are poison for you
Change the seasons to flourish and be free
Arise, my love, for now you must march with me.

I fixed my gaze on Kaifi, convinced that he had written this poem for me, and I alone had the right to march with him. I was stubborn, proud, headstrong, and always ready to raise my voice against a perceived injustice. It became clear to me that only a man with progressive views about women could be my husband. I recalled that I was just thirteen when Abbajan was transferred from Hyderabad to Aurangabad and the entire family had moved there to join him. My younger sister Sardar, my brother Chote Bhaijan and I were taking our exams, and were left behind in Hyderabad with a maid to look after us. When it was time for us to join our parents Chote Bhaijan who had antiquated views, stipulated that he would chaperone us on the condition that we wore burqahs. This was quite ridiculous! How could either of us have owned a burqah, when our older sisters did not? Adamant, I pronounced, 'I will not wear a burqah; I do not own one.' My younger sister, who was very good-natured, compromised, saying, 'Bhaijan, I do not have a burqah but I shall go with you wearing a chadar.' I dug my heels in, 'I am not even willing to wear a chadar... not under any circumstances. You take Sardar. When Abbajan returns I shall go with him.' My brother was made of equally stubborn stuff; he went off with Sardar, leaving me behind with the maid as my sole companion. When Abbajan heard that I was on my own he came post-haste to take me home; but he did not chide me or complain of the inconvenience caused to him.

I was a headstrong young woman who, over the slightest disagreement with Ammajan, would go without food for days. Abbajan was the only person who could cajole me into eating. Kaifi's poem *Aurat* stirred my independent spirit and made it clear to me that I would find it impossible to spend my life with a conservative man.

2

Making My Own Choices

After the conference, Akhtar Bhai suggested that Sultana Apa and the three poets Sardar Jafri, Majrooh Sultanpuri and Kaifi Azmi should visit the Ajanta and Ellora caves near Aurangabad. All of us hopped on a train from Hyderabad to Aurangabad, an overnight journey of some three hundred miles. Our carriage was packed with other passengers and their luggage. Some of us found seats, but Akhtar Bhai, Zakia, Kaifi and I had to stand for part of the journey. I was standing at some distance from Kaifi when, quite suddenly, the train lurched to a halt and I was tipped into his arms. Kaifi steadied me gently, holding me as though I were a flower. I felt a rush of colour to my face and stepped back; people had begun to whisper about us but quite frankly, I could not have cared less.

At Aurangabad, Abbajan and all my siblings were waiting for us. We were made comfortable in our rooms and after we had rested, and feasted at Ammajan's sumptuous table, we set off for Ajanta, a distance of some sixty miles from Aurangabad. Abbajan had a car and he commandeered another from a friend. I made sure I was in the same car as Kaifi. He sat in the front with Sardar Bhai, Sultana Apa, Majrooh and I sat in the back. Majrooh and Kaifi kept us entertained throughout the journey. Majrooh parodied his own popular film song:

I'll not let you go
I'll leave dogs in your tow
I'll blind your eyes
I'll break your legs…

And so on. Kaifi mimicked the old Lucknow poets. Occasionally, he would look back at me through half-open eyes. I found everything about him irresistibly attractive and could feel myself being drawn into his charmed world.

In Ajanta, Kaifi and I maintained a distance because we knew that Choti Apajan had us under surveillance. Our party spent the night in a dak bungalow and the following morning we went to see Panchakki Bibi's mausoleum. Prince Azam Shah, a son of the Mughal Emperor Aurangzeb, had this built for his mother, Dilras Bano Begum Rabia Durrani. It is a replica of the Taj Mahal, except that it is not made of white marble. Everyone was busy walking around and looking at the monuments when I spotted a forlorn Kaifi standing under a tree. Quietly, I walked up to him. Grief-stricken, he said, 'Soon, I'll go away and we will never meet again. In any case, why would it matter to you; you have been avoiding me.' I could not bring myself to say anything. Scuffing the earth with my big toe, I kept my eyes fixed to the ground. I did not want Kaifi to see my tears. He continued, 'With your permission, I would like to dedicate a poem to you…' I nodded, and even though my head was lowered, I knew that Kaifi's eyes were fixed on me, as he began to recite.

You

You are the personification of refinement and charm
You are not just the spring but the prize of spring
You are the garden concealed in a bud…

I hurried away, unable to stop my eyes from brimming over.

In the evening, everyone assembled for tea, and not long after the moon rose. Some of us got together and made up a game, in which one person who was 'the captive' was given the task of summing up everybody else's character in one word. I cannot remember the exact rules of the game, but I remember well that Kaifi's name for me was 'Magnet'. Three days after the picnic, Sardar Bhai, Sultana Apa and Majrooh returned to Bombay but Kaifi decided to stay on in Aurangabad. He had struck up a friendship with my younger sisters and even Abbajan found him quite pleasant company. Both my older brothers and Choti Apajan, however, disapproved of our growing closeness and hounded us like vigilantes. If they spotted us sitting together one of them would come over and sit between us.

One day, I finished lunch before the others and went to Kaifi's room where he was sitting by himself. 'You should get married to the Bombay girl and everything will be fine,' I advised him.

Kaifi replied, 'I am willing to do anything you ask of me, but if you say, "Get married to a bottle of oil" that is unlikely!'

Suppressing a giggle, I said, 'Well, then show me your hand.' Kaifi extended his right hand towards me and I took it into mine. Tenderly, I traced his line of fate with my index finger and said, 'You will have a love marriage.'

'Really?' asked Kaifi looking at me.

'Yes' I continued, 'the star under your index finger indicates this.' I picked up a piece of paper and wrote on it, 'With you by my side, life will pass by like the morning breeze caressing flowers.' As I turned around and handed the paper to Kaifi, his eyes held my gaze, and just as he was saying, 'I can see my destiny in your eyes,' we heard some voices and I slipped away.

Ammajan heard of our growing attraction to each other and reprimanded me. In no uncertain terms she forbade me to go near Kaifi's room again. My mother's stand strengthened my brothers' resolve and they locked the doors to the inter-connecting room between Kaifi's room and mine. My siblings did not dare confront me because I was known for my sharp tongue; but in Ammajan's presence I had to hold my peace. My two younger sisters, Qamar and Zafar were devoted to me, and in their eyes I could do no wrong. As I would lie sobbing on my bed, each would hold me tight, in turn and say, 'Allah, Apa Bi how absolutely wonderful it would be if you were to marry Kaifi Bhai; we could brag to our friends that Kaifi Azmi is our brother-in-law!'

One morning, to my horror, I discovered that a tearful Kaifi had left for Bombay—he had not been permitted to say goodbye to me. I was distraught because I had no address for him. By the evening I was desperate and rushed into his room, which was completely bare. I was about to give up all hope when I spotted some papers on Kaifi's bedside table. Instantly, I scooped them up. Flicking through the pages of a writing pad I found a beautiful poem entitled, *For Shaukat.* At the bottom of the page was his Bombay address: Raj Bhavan, Sandhurst Road, Bombay 22. I sank into the nearest chair; I had been given a new lease of life. After I had recovered my equilibrium I was able to read the poem.

> *My nights were longing for the moon*
> *I swear by your brow, you are that moon*
> *I roamed gardens searching for a flower*
> *I swear by your flushed brow, you are that flower*
> *My poetry was seeking a magical song*
> *I have found that song in your spellbinding gaze.*

Alas, I cannot recall the entire poem, but I was deeply moved. As if in a daze, I ran up to the rooftop where, away from prying eyes I wrote to Kaifi with complete abandon.

Kaifi, I love you boundlessly. No power in the world can stop me coming to you; no mountain, no river, no sea, no people, no sky, no angel, no God; and God alone knows what else.

Yours and only yours,
Shaukat.

Akbar, who was my late Chacha's son, lived with us; he was a sensitive and affectionate young man who liked Kaifi and understood our predicament. He offered to help, and I gave Kaifi Akbar's school address. Within five or six days I received Kaifi's reply. To this day I remember some parts of it.

Shaukat, my own Shaukat,
I received your letter. Each syllable was like the first drops of rain falling on parched earth.

An exchange of letters began between us. Every day, Akbar brought me Kaifi's letters; at times six, at others even a dozen. Each letter began with a poem dedicated to me, followed by a poignant text. I would go to the rooftop, and read the letters over and over again. I would write him six or seven letters a day. Kaifi was a member of the Communist Party of India and lived in a commune where every comrade's mail was pinned on a board for collection. My letters became a source of entertainment for the comrades, who teased Kaifi when they saw that every day he received six or seven letters written in the same hand, and enclosed in similar envelopes.

All too soon, the day arrived when my family discovered what was going on and placed restrictions on all fronts. With Akbar's complicity I continued to receive Kaifi's letters but my letters did not reach him. Apart from Abbajan and my two younger sisters I had no allies in the family. The battle lines were drawn; all the peons were with Bare Bhaijan and Chote Bhaijan, but the kamatan who helped in the house, was in my camp. She would conceal my letters under the newspapers lining the basket in which she took the maize for grinding and smuggle them out. Inevitably, my brothers discovered this; they intercepted my letters and tore them to shreds. To complicate matters, Usman, my maternal cousin to whom I was betrothed, arrived on the scene. One day he brandished Abbajan's revolver and threatened to shoot himself; another day he took the poison nila thotha. Bare Bhaijan and company had to rush him to the hospital where he was treated and recovered. There was pandemonium as the entire household was turned upside down.

Twenty days passed and Kaifi did not hear from me. He assumed that I was upset about something he might have written. Kaifi wrote to me in his blood.

21 March, Night. 1 a.m.

After I finished writing to you I sealed the envelope and went to bed thinking I might get some sleep, but could not. I re-read your letter and was unable to control my tears. Shaukat, it is my misfortune that you have no faith in me or in my love. For days I have been thinking of nothing but ways of trying to convince you that I love you. I have taken a blade and cut a deep wound into my wrist and now I am writing to you in my blood. For months I have shed tears for our love and now I am shedding my blood. I do not know what the future holds for us.

Moti, he continued, addressing me by the name I was called by my family, *I am deeply hurt. How could you write, "Now I know that his eyes are not on me but on someone else who does not understand him; nor does she want to understand him"? Take back these words, Shaukat, and do not mock my love. If you cannot do anything for me, so be it. Even as I started loving you, I knew there was no hope. God will look after me. You question my love and my intention to marry you. All I can say is that one day, I shall prove myself to you and to the world.*

My Shuakat, what is to become of me and of my love? We are so far away from each other that it is impossible for you to see the my pain. You believe what others have to say without trying to understand my compulsions. If I have said anything to upset you, please forgive me.

Lots and lots of love,
Yours
Kaifi

To this day I have the letter. When I read it my head began to reel. I decided that the time had come for me to do some plain speaking. I took the letter to Abbajan, and declared that I would marry none other than Kaifi.

Abbajan, who was first and foremost a friend to all his children, read Kaifi's letter, smiled and said, 'Betey, a poet has a way with words that can sound terribly romantic but it is hardly wise to take him seriously. He may well be lying under the shade of a tree, enjoying the gentle breeze, as he claims, "I am hitting my head against a wall in agony and am writing to you in my blood," as he dips his pen in the blood of a goat! Let us wait and watch.'

When Kaifi did not hear from me he was miserable and wept inconsolably. Everyone in the Party felt his pain. Comrade Mirza Ashfaq Beg, a lawyer who, apart from being a Party wholetimer, also worked with the English newspaper *The New Age*, decided to intervene. He appealed to P.C. Joshi, the General Secretary of the Party and it was with official approval that Comrade Beg arrived in Aurangabad and presented himself at Abbajan's office, as a C.I.D. (Criminal Investigation Division) officer, who had come from Delhi, especially to meet Yahya Khan. Abbajan had him ushered in immediately. In time, Comrade Beg revealed his true identity. I do not know what transpired between them, but I do know that Abbajan came home and asked Ammajan, 'Please, lay on a special meal as I have an important guest with me.' Mirza Ashfaq Beg did not give up till he had convinced Abbajan that there was some merit in my marrying Kaifi.

That same night, I am told that Abbajan said to Ammajan, 'Bibi, it is unlikely that you and I shall live forever. If we get Moti married to some boy she does not care for, then within three months of the wedding she will return home. And when you and I are no longer around, what will become of her? Who will look after her? But if we marry her off to Kaifi, she will have to assume responsibility for her choice: make or break, she will not be able to blame us and will have to live her own life.' Ammajan heard him out silently but did not respond.

Later that evening Abbajan spoke to me in confidence, 'I am taking you to Bombay without telling your mother and siblings. Once you have seen their lifestyle for yourself, you will have to make your own decision. If you decide that is how you would like to live your life, I shall get you married off without consulting anybody.' I was delirious with joy and rushed off to pack my suitcase. Abbajan explained to the family, 'Moti is very distraught these days; I am taking her along on tour; it will give her an opportunity to think in peace about what is good for her.'

When Abbajan went on tour a mobile kitchen accompanied him in the shape of an innovative trunk. It opened out as a small cupboard with shelves for all the spices, lentils, rice, other dry rations and the kitchen utensils. Ammajan wanted to send the trunk with Abbajan, but he stopped her, saying 'There is no need for it because we shall be back in a couple of days.' The peon had bought our train tickets for Bombay. As I stepped out of my childhood home, I looked at it tearfully, as I said under my breath, *Khush raho ahl-e-chaman ham to safar kar chale* (Keep well, people of my land, for I must travel.)

3

Living in a Commune

As the train approached Bombay my heart began to pound. The acrid smoke from the factories, the rancid odours of hordes of human beings, the squalor of the city and terrifying sounds of the trains assaulted my senses. I asked Abbajan, 'How do people here survive without oxygen?' This was my first encounter with a big city. I had passed through Delhi once, on the way to my ancestral home in Saharanpur Lohari for Bare Bhaijan's wedding, but somehow the capital had not made much of an impression on me. Abbajan and I got off the train at Bori Bandar station and took a taxi directly to the Sea View Hotel where we deposited our bags and freshened up. I took care to wear attractive clothes and sat down to a light meal with Abbajan.

At around five o'clock in the evening we arrived at Raj Bhavan, the Communist Party office on Sandhurst Road. I remained in the taxi while Abbajan went inside, returning shortly with a rather good looking young man who was smiling even as he sized me up discreetly. He said, 'I'm Mehdi. Kaifi hasn't arrived as yet; he lives in the Andheri commune. Please make yourselves comfortable in the office upstairs while I contact him on the telephone. It should not take him more than two hours to get here.' I was exhausted and said, 'I think we should go back to our hotel, when Kaifi returns, please send him there.'

'Very well', said Mehdi. Abbajan and I headed back to our hotel in a taxi. Over the din of the city I could hear the song *Ghunghat ke pat khol ri, tohe piya milein ge* (Lift up your veil; you will meet your beloved), probably from a radio in some wayside cafe. At the hotel, I took myself to bed in an attempt to get some rest and Abbajan occupied himself with a newspaper.

At around seven o'clock Kaifi arrived with Mehdi and Abbajan opened the door for them. When I saw Kaifi my eyes brimmed over and he too, seemed in a daze. He had never quite believed that I would actually turn up in Bombay with my father. Mehdi laughed and said, 'Kaifi was almost run over by a motor car when he heard that you had arrived.' Both Kaifi and he asked in unison, 'Why are you staying in a hotel?' And added, 'Bannay Bhai and Razia Apa have invited you to their place. You must move to Sikri Bhavan tomorrow morning. We shall come over to fetch you.' Bannay Bhai was Sajjad Zaheer, the General Secretary of the Progressive Writers' Movement, and Razia Apa was his wife. Kaifi was looking at me through half closed eyes because he did not want anybody to notice but every fibre of my being was aware of his presence. Mehdi and Kaifi sat chatting with Abbajan till midnight. Promising to return the following morning they left to catch some sleep; for me though, there was none. I was in a new world with new people but I had just one thought in my mind, that I would marry Kaifi and nobody but Kaifi.

I was up early. After my bath I changed into my best clothes, a saffron kurta and dupatta with a white shalwar. I looked in the mirror; I was looking good. Abbajan offered his prayers and as we were finishing breakfast Kaifi arrived. This time he was alone and joined us for some tea. As he was loading our bags into the taxi, Kaifi whispered to me, 'You look like a spring flower.' We headed off for No. 7 Sikri Bhavan, on Walkeshwar Road, where we were led to a rather spacious living room, which reflected simple good taste. Bannay Bhai and Razia Apa greeted us with the warmth of a longstanding friendship. Their two delightful little daughters, Najma and Mona were hanging around curiously. Razia Apa laughed and said, 'I am so pleased to see you; because Kaifi's tears would most certainly have ruined my carpet.' When Kaifi had stopped receiving my letters it was Razia Apa who much like an affectionate older sister, comforted him as he lay weeping into her carpet. What struck me most about these people was that not one of them mocked Kaifi and me. They did not try to shame us or unsettle us with disapproving looks. In fact, everyone was most sympathetic and accommodating. How different this was from the world I had left behind, where people lacked compassion and were quick to draw attention to what they considered a human weakness. My first impression of Kaifi's friends strengthened my resolve to marry him. Razia Apa announced that tea was being served and added, 'You shouldn't have gone to a hotel but come directly to us.' Abbajan believed—like many other people – that tea was an unhealthy beverage, particularly for young girls as it was supposed to darken their complexions. Consequently, I never drank tea, but sitting in 7 Sikri Bhavan I picked up my cup and sipped its contents as if it were nectar from the gods.

Later that evening Bannay Bhai suggested, 'Let's go to the Hanging Gardens,' which were barely a furlong from their house. We set off with Bannay Bhai leading the way, as he tried to reassure Abbajan, 'Once Moti is married to Kaifi all will be well. Kaifi's mind will be at rest and all your worries will be over.' Abbajan kept nodding and saying, 'Yes, yes.' Walking behind them, Sardar Bhai, Razia Apa, Mirza Ashfaq Beg, Mehdi, Kaifi and I arrived at the Naz restaurant, where coffee was ordered for all of us. As I looked out towards the bay, the sun was setting and the street lamps had been lit. It looked as if the sea had spread its arms out to take the entire city into its embrace, and was wearing a diamond necklace that glittered and sparkled like my life. I lost myself in dreams of an enchanted future.

The following morning Abbajan and I set off with Kaifi, taking a local train to the Andheri commune. I felt I had arrived in some hill station like Matheran. Katthal, banana and mango trees stood with giant banyans. A swing was hanging from one of the trees and the air was filled with the scent of mogra and juhi. A few years earlier, this idyllic setting had been the home of the Cultural Squad, a wing of the Communist Party. Many artists and dancers had lived here, among whom were Sachin Shankar, the choreographer who was Uday Shankar's paternal cousin; Gill, Dina Pathak, and Prem Dhawan. In 1943, during the Bengal Famine, artists from the Communist Party of India had toured the length and breadth of the country and collected two lakh rupees for relief work. Their theme song, *Bhuka hai Bengal* (Bengal is hungry), written by Wamiq Jaunpuri, became very well known throughout India.

We went to Kaifi's tiny room in which there was a loosely strung jute charpai with a dhurrie, a mattress, a sheet and a pillow. In one corner, there was a chair and a small table on which there were some books, piles of newspapers, a mug and a glass. The simplicity of this room touched my heart and I thought, 'Just you wait, little room I shall lavish such love on you that your destiny will change.'

Lunch in the commune was unlike anything I had seen. Everyone had an aluminum plate, two bowls, and two low wooden chaukis (one for sitting on and the other to use as an improvised table). The cook served the food, which was a daal, a vegetable, four chapattis with ghee, some rice, salt, onions, a slice of lemon, and I think, some pickle on the side. Everyone washed their own utensils and put them away. I was watching Abbajan's every move, anxious that he might take umbrage and ask me to return with him to Hyderabad. I saw him bristle and it was obvious that he found it distasteful to eat out of metal dishes. After a few mouthfuls Abbajan rose quietly, adding under his breath, 'I will not wash these.' I rushed to pick up his plates, washed them with mine and put them back where they belonged.

We returned to Bannay Bhai's house and had not been there long when Abbajan suggested, 'Why don't you get dressed and we'll go for a stroll along the Chowpatty beach.' I got dressed with trepidation and we set off. Abbajan looked very contemplative, 'Betey, now that you've seen how they live, have you made a decision? Do you still wish to marry Kaifi or would you rather return with me? Remember, in our family marriage is a commitment for life: a girl only leaves her husband's home when she dies. You will not be able to return home to us and say, "Kaifi Sahib's feet are too big, I don't like them or that he is a 'whole-timer' with the Party and does not earn more than forty rupees a month; I want a divorce for some reason or another." I stopped in my tracks and turned to face my father, 'Abbajan, these are good people. At least Kaifi is a whole-timer, but were he a labourer I would still have married him and carried baskets of earth on my head. My decision is irrevocable. God willing, I shall never give you cause to reproach me.' Reassured, Abbajan returned to the Sikri Bhavan and said to Bannay Bhai, 'Please arrange their nikah for tomorrow; I have come away without formal leave and must head back.' Now that the date and time for my marriage to Kaifi were fixed; my heart began to race ahead of itself. I lay awake the whole night, thinking, 'Tomorrow I shall begin a completely new life.'

The news of our marriage created a buzz in the Party. Comrade Ghate, the tight-fisted Party Treasurer, who was as short as he was lean and mean, grudgingly parted with a hundred rupees, saying, 'What guarantee do we have that this Laila Majnun drama will not come to an end in four months and the Party will have incurred an unnecessary loss of a hundred rupees.' The comrades burst out laughing! How could they have known that this particular drama was not going to end, not even after fifty-five years.

The following morning, I was sitting on the carpet with Razia Apa who was applying henna on my palms when I began to weep. Bannay Bhai who was lying on the divan nearby with what I suspect may have been a slight temperature, said to me, 'I say, you girls are rather odd. You are getting married to someone you have chosen, what earthly reason do you have to cry? Surely, you should be happy and smiling!' I was missing home and my mother, although Razia Apa was as affectionate as Ammajan would have been. She had taken out her wedding clothes for me: a kurta with zari embroidery, a gharara and a dupatta with gota. She made me wear her gold bangles and added the final touch by slipping a gold band from Kaifi on my ring finger.

In the evening, at about four o'clock, Mehdi and Munish brought Qazi Marghay from Bhendi Bazar. The house was packed with people. I think nearly all the progressive writers in Bombay had gathered, including Josh Malihabadi, Majaz, Krishan Chandar, Mahendernath, Sahir, Patras Bukhari and his younger brother Zulfiqar Bukhari (who was the Director of the Bombay Radio Station), Riffat Sarosh, Vishwamitra Adil, Sikandar Ali Wajd, who was a judge in Aurangabad, Ismat Chughtai, Sardar Jafri and Sultana Apa. Sikandar Ali Wajd and Sardar Bhai were the witnesses and according to custom, they entered the room where I was sitting and asked me, 'Do you consent to a nikah with Athar Hussain Rizvi, son of Fatch Hussain Rizvi?' It was then that I learnt Kaifi's real name.

I was told that when, as a matter of form, the qazi asked the bridegroom's religion, a hushed silence descended on all present because Kaifi was Shi'a and I, Sunni. In such marriages it is customary to have two qazis or else some orthodox mullahs do not consider the nikah valid. The poor Party was always strapped for funds, and I am not too sure how Comrade Ghate would have responded to a demand for another hundred rupees! Bannay Bhai smiled and responded, '...religion Hanafi', which is one of the schools of Sunni jurisprudence. Josh Sahib stared at Bannay Bhai with a questioning, 'Hunh?' and was about to object when Bannay Bhai winked at him to signal that he hold his peace.

With the nikah over, Kaifi and I were husband and wife. I was feeling shy and, in keeping with obligatory behaviour for brides in those days, was sitting with downcast eyes when Sultana Apa announced, 'Moti, Ismat is here.' I admired Ismat Apa's work and was keen to see her. I looked up immediately, forgetting bridal propriety, much to the amusement of the women present.

Sultana Apa took my hand and led me out to the verandah where the men were sitting. I removed the garland of jasmine flowers but kept my head covered like a new bride. Majaz recited *Aaj ki Raat*

(Tonight) and Josh Sahib a rubai. Following a popular convention at weddings, Mehdi and Munish decided to get up to some mischief and announced, 'Josh Sahib, according to a Hyderabadi custom stardust is rubbed on the bridegroom's father's head, and at the moment you are standing in for Kaifi's father.' The poor lamb acquiesced, and everyone was hugely entertained watching Mehdi, Mirza Ashfaq Beg, Munish and others cover Josh Sahib's pate with stardust, as barfi and laddus were passed around. It was a splendid evening and a propitious beginning to our new life.

The manuscript of Kaifi's book *Akhir-e-Shab* (The End of Night) was awaiting publication. Overnight, Sardar Bhai had a copy printed and bound in beautiful brown leather, and presented it to me. He inscribed an extract from Kaifi's poem *Aurat* for me.

Woman

Patience will not help you struggle through life
Blood, not tears, sustains the pulse of life
You will fly when you're free and not ensnared by love
Heaven is not just in the arms of a man
Walk unfettered on the path of freedom with me
Arise, my love, for now you must march with me.

I could not hold back my tears when I saw that Kaifi had dedicated the book to me: 'To "S", *In solitude I have brought my craft to the end of night; if you join me it will be dawn.* Kaifi'

The day after our wedding Josh Sahib's lady friend gave me two rupees for munh dikhai (the custom of 'seeing' the bride for the first time), which I accepted quite happily. Josh Sahib was very impressed by Abbajan, as was Bannay Bhai who declared, 'We would be hard pressed to find another such progressive and reasonable man in this day and age.' When Kaifi and I went to see Abbajan off at the Victoria Terminus Railway Station, he was very quiet and thoughtful. Just as his train was about to pull out of the station Abbajan said, 'I have solved your problem but my problem has yet to be resolved.

Now, I have to face my wife.' My heart went out to Abbajan, because although my mother was a devoted wife she did not forgive or forget easily. When Abbajan told her of my marriage to Kaifi, Ammajan did not speak to him for over a month.

After Abbajan's train pulled out of the station, Kaifi and I took a local train to Andheri station from where we hired a victoria home. The fare from the station to the commune for this horse drawn carriage was just one rupee. At home, I looked at the frugal disarray of our room and decided to get down to work. I threw out the charpai and after giving the room a good sweep I dusted Kaifi's books. I spread some newspapers on the floor and put the mattress on them to make our new bed. I put the chair in a corner and near it I set up the small table and kept Kaifi's books on it. I used Kaifi's glass as a vase and polished the aluminum mug till it shone. Kaifi sat silently, watching me for a while and then he said, 'I cannot believe my good fortune. I could not have imagined that you will be mine; no, not even in my wildest dreams.'

Kaifi was the editor of the Party quarterly, *Naya Adab* and had to get back to work but I continued to tidy our room. I tore up a sari and converted it into a curtain. Next, I sat down and made a list of things that I thought were necessary to make our room more comfortable and attractive. Abbajan had given us five hundred rupees, which was all the money he had on him, because he was certain that I would return to Hyderabad with him.

ঙ৬

I was up at dawn and decided to step out and inspect the commune. In the courtyard, a large tea kettle was simmering on a stove and the comrades were sitting around it, sipping tea, engrossed in their newspapers. However, when one of them spotted me, he said, 'Hello Comrade', and withdrew behind his newspaper. Comrade Mirza Ashfaq Beg was absorbed in reading the news and savouring his morning tea, blissfully unaware that his pyjama was torn in several places. I asked for an extra mug and took back two mugs of tea to our room. I woke Kaifi up gently, and we sat together drinking our tea. I discovered that Kaifi could not start his day without a cup of tea and I, who had never drunk tea in my life, instantly acquired my husband's habit. I decided that what I needed most was a teapot, cups, saucers, and at least a tray and a tea-cosy because this was how tea was served in my home.

The commune was a completely new experience for me. Surrounded by tall, dense banyan and katthal trees, it was a charmed world but even more charming were the people who lived in it. They were enlightened and humane individuals who were struggling to create a new world for the poor, the destitute and the hungry. Although they were from different parts of India, these people were like one family where everyone was addressed as 'Comrade', which at the time meant an evolved human being. In the commune breakfast was an important ritual which the comrades shared in the dining room before setting off on the tasks assigned to them by the Party. They did not return home till the evening.

Every Sunday, the Progressive writers in the city met at Bannay Bhai's house and read from their work, which was then discussed by everyone. The meetings usually went on till the evening. Never failing in her hospitality, Razia Apa ensured that all those who attended the meetings were served tea. Nobody dared to be absent as Bannay Bhai kept his eye on everyone—especially on Kaifi and me. Often, on our way back from Bannay Bhai's house, Kaifi and I would head off for a stroll along the Chowpatty. Laughing and eating corn on the cob, we revelled in each other's love.

One Sunday, I had a sudden urge to see a film and when I put this to Kaifi, he agreed readily, regardless of the fact that he did not have more than two and a half rupees in his pocket. Chetan Anand's film *Safar* was playing at the Roxy Cinema on Charni Road, which was a mile away from 7 Sikri Bhavan. We walked to the cinema well in time for the three o'clock show and bought two tickets, at one rupee and four annas each. During the intermission I felt thirsty, but in those days all public taps were turned off in the afternoon. On a footpath near the Roxy, an old woman sat with an earthenware pot, selling water at two paisas a glass. Kaifi suggested, 'Why don't you drink a glass of water, tell the old woman that you're getting the money from your husband and then just run off.' I did as he said. For many years whenever we passed by the Opera House Kaifi would remind me, 'That old woman is waiting for you and she wants her two paisas.' That evening we missed the meeting and consequently, the following day we were taken to task by Bannay Bhai, who said, 'You were absent from the meeting yesterday; in future, please remember that this is unacceptable.' Kaifi attempted to make some feeble excuse, but I could barely suppress my smile and had to leave the room.

In 1947 both Progressive Writers and conventional poets participated in mushairas, but it was the Progressive poets who brought the house down, as cries of 'vah vah' would resonate in the hall. Progressive poetry was different from conventional romantic poetry and was popular because of its engagement with politics and the lives of ordinary people. This was new poetry which was not about the nightingale and the rose, but about the migrant, the clerk, the alienated, mothers struggling in their homes, and life on the footpath. The Progressive poets were appreciated not just for their choice of subjects but also for their style of recitation. Amongst the Progressive poets were Josh Malihabadi, Sardar Jafri, Kaifi Azmi, Sahir Ludhianvi, Majrooh Sultanpuri and others, but amongst the traditional poets the only name I can recall is Saghar Nizami's. The day after a mushaira everyone would gather at Bannay Bhai's place where he would say in his singular style, 'Vah! Last night, our lads stole the show!' In the decades of the 1940s and 1950s people in India understood Urdu more than they do today. Alas!

◌⚬◌

Soon after we were married, Kaifi was reciting his poem *Haqiqaten* (Realities) at a mushaira as though under a spell. When he reached the stanza,

My friend and protector
Whose youth is a testament to suffering
Conceals her sighs behind a smile
And shields me from harm, although
I have nothing to offer her but regret.

Many people turned around to look at me, and found me rather well turned out and sitting pretty. I felt quite self-conscious because their enquiring eyes seemed to ask, 'Is this the beloved whose stricken youth is a testament to suffering?' Kaifi's poem was very well received, and the following day Bannay Bhai said to me, 'Moti, last night your husband stole the show!'

Gradually, it became quite clear to me that Kaifi's world was in complete contrast to the world I had left behind in Hyderabad. I saw that people in the commune cared not only for those who were close to them, but they were concerned about the world and all humanity. They did not worry about their immediate families as much as they did about the workers, the peasants and the labouring classes. Their aim in life was to free the weak from the cruel oppression of the exploitative capitalist system.

After our marriage the first present that Kaifi gave me was a book called, *The Evolution of Man*. As I read it, I could feel the cobwebs clinging to my brain, because of my bourgeois Hyderabadi lifestyle, gradually clearing away. I was becoming receptive to progressive ideas, especially because I saw the comrades working hard without any thought of personal gain. I wanted to help, and decided that by taking an interest in the comrades' diet, I would contribute towards improving their health. I discussed this with Sultana Apa, who agreed readily. We decided that when the comrades came home that evening we would serve them a new menu. I announced, 'I make an excellent alu ka bhurta', Sultana Apa added, 'I can make gur ke mithey chaval.' We went to the kitchen and consulted our cook, a mild tempered man from the hills, who encouraged us, saying, 'You must try your hand.'

I boiled heaps of potatoes, mashed them, added salt, coriander and chopped green chilies, and foolishly started blending the ingredients with my right hand. I felt I had touched live coals and watched my hand turn red as it began to swell! Poor Kaifi smiled gently as he applied oil to my wounds and fanned them. If this were not disaster enough, Sultana Apa rushed into my room looking defeated. 'Moti,' she cried, 'it's a catastrophe! The comrades will be here any minute and the rice is nowhere near being cooked.' Nursing my hand, I rushed back to the kitchen. I realized it would be difficult, well nigh impossible for the rice to soften in the gur syrup; so I suggested, 'Let's strain the rice and separate it from the syrup; boil it in water to soften it; strain it again, add the syrup and sprinkle it with some essence of kevra and desiccated coconut.' Mercifully, the recipe worked. The comrades were delighted with the transformation in their food. Emboldened, I made koftas after consulting Ismat Apa. There was no end to the comrades' joy as they cheered, 'Long live, Comrade Moti, Long live Comrade Moti!' I was overjoyed at this vote of appreciation.

Three months after we were married, on the fifteenth of August 1947, we celebrated the long awaited day of India's independence. From the early hours of the morning there was a buzz of activity in the Commune as all the comrades bathed and put on their finest clothes. We gathered at the Party Headquarters at eight o'clock. The tricolour was hoisted and unfurled as slogans filled the air, 'Long Live the Revolution!' 'Long Live Indian Independence!' 'Long Live Mother India!' and 'Death to the British Raj!' The celebrations began with Majaz reciting his song, *Bol ari o dharti bol* (Speak! O earth, speak up!) Sardar Jafri recited a revolutionary poem as did Kaifi. Beautiful young girls from the Party cadre, including Dina Pathak and her sister Tarla sang *Sarey jahan say achcha Hindustan hamara* (In the whole wide world our Hindustan is incomparable!) Set to music by Ravi Shankar the anthem was written by the poet Iqbal. It is ironic that many Pakistanis now claim Iqbal as the person who first dreamt of a separate Muslim state in South Asia. P.C. Joshi, Sajjad Zaheer and others made speeches, after which we formed a procession; and I, a lissom young girl joined in with

Kaifi's hand in mine as we began to march forward with dreams of a free India in our eyes.

The procession stopped at Gowalia Tank, where there were more speeches, singing, dancing, sloganeering and cheering. I returned to my room and fell asleep, exhausted. However, Sardar Bhai, Zoe Ansari, Mirza Ashfaq Beg, Mehdi and Munish roamed the city. They went into an Irani teashop, where a large portrait of George V was hanging on the wall. Sardar Bhai climbed onto a table, took the picture off the wall and flung it on the floor. The hapless proprietor tried his best to restrain Sardar Bhai even though he was a trifle scared of the fervour of the young men. Zoe Ansari reproached Sardar Bhai who lost his temper and planted a resounding slap on poor Zoe's face, stunning him into silence. By the time the comrades returned, news of their antics and particularly of Sardar Bhai's action had reached the Commune, but he remained unruffled. Feelings were running high and members of the Communist Party wanted to obliterate every sign of the British Raj.

Soon after independence news of blood curdling communal riots began pouring in. Each time I heard about the atrocities, my heart would sink. P.C. Joshi had to issue an order that no comrade should go be seen in a shervani, as this was associated in some people's minds with Muslims, although it was also worn by many Hindus, including Jawaharlal Nehru, the Prime Minister of India. To diffuse the communal madness that had overtaken their compatriots and in the hope of refashioning a new India, the Communist Party set up IPTA, The Indian People's Theatre Association, as an autonomous organization. Sardar Jafri, Anil d'Silva, Mulk Raj Anand, Khwaja Ahmed Abbas were among its founding members. It soon attracted some of the best names in the business such as Balraj Sahni, his brother Bhisham Sahni, and Prem Dhawan, who had come to Bombay from Lahore, which was now in Pakistan. Dina Pathak, Khwaja Ahmed Abbas Sahib's wife Mujji, Mohan Sehgal, Vishwamitra Adil and many others worked together to stage plays that promoted communal harmony. Prithvi Theatre had already been established and could well have been considered a rival concern but Prithvi Raj Kapoor was the Honorary President of IPTA. Uzra Butt and Zohra Sehgal from Prithvi Theatre also joined as honorary members. How I long to find such unity in theatre groups today.

Though sympathetic to the Party's concerns, I was lost in my own world where my primary concern was that tea must be drunk with utmost propriety. One morning, I was sitting in my room embroidering a tea cosy when P.C. Joshi, the General Secretary of the Communist Party, walked into our room. He was wearing khaki shorts and a white short-sleeved shirt. I had never seen him at such close quarters; he was dark complexioned and attractive, with a genial and compassionate face. I was completely unprepared for his visit and stood up, partly in astonishment. He asked me to sit down, and I did. 'What do you do the whole day?' he asked. I was overcome with shyness but managed to say, 'Nothing'. He smiled and said, 'The wife of a communist should never sit idle; she should involve herself alongside her husband with the work of the Party; she should earn money, and afterwards, when she has children, she should raise them as good citizens; only then can she claim the right to be the wife of a worthy communist.' He spoke with such gentle sympathy that his words made a strong impression on me. I decided that I should earn money to support myself. I was not a Party member and Kaifi had to pay an extra thirty rupees a month for my food. As a whole-timer it was very difficult for him to find the time to earn a livelihood, but he had little choice. He started writing a column for an Urdu daily, *Jumhuriat*. The poor darling had to wake up every morning at five o'clock, sit under a tree and think up a new subject, day after day. It pained me to see him struggle so, but I was in no position to help.

That evening, when Kaifi returned home, I informed him of my decision. Kaifi smiled encouragingly but wondered where I would find a job, as I was just a matriculate. I had given the matter some thought and said, 'I used to take part in the annual plays at school, and I am sure I can participate in radio plays, and I have a good enough singing voice to sing in a chorus.'

'Well then,' said Kaifi, 'I shall take you to the Radio Station tomorrow. My friend Dubey directs radio plays there.' This was the same V.K. Dubey who went on to become the General Manager of HMV. My audition was successful, and I earned ten rupees for my work. I felt I had struck gold!

Prem Dhawan, who worked for the Party and also wrote film songs was a kindly soul. I asked him to find me some work. He was surprised and asked, 'You want to work?'

I responded 'And why not?' adding, 'I have a good voice; if nothing else, at least I can sing in a chorus.'

'All right then, come with me tomorrow morning at ten o'clock. I am rehearsing one of my songs with Burman Da,' he said, referring to S.D. Burman, the legendary film music composer. The following morning, I went with Prem Dhawan and his fiancée Noor, who had a good voice and sang in a chorus. I do not remember which theatre we went to, it might have been in Dadar, but when we walked in, we saw a handsome young man rehearsing a song. Later I learnt he was the famous singer Mukesh. Burman Da approved of my voice, but I had to rehearse for two days. After the recording I was paid thirty rupees. I could not believe that I had earned money through my own hard work, and to this day I find it difficult to explain the significance of those thirty rupees in my life. As word got around that I wanted to work, I began to get offers for dubbing, for which I was paid two hundred and at times even five hundred rupees.

Not much later Muji Abbas, who was a particularly attractive woman, dropped by to see me. She asked me quite casually, 'Would you be willing to work for IPTA?' Trying to hide my excitement I asked, 'What work?' She explained, 'Ismat Apa has written a one-act play, *Dhani Bankein* (Green Bangles), on the Hindu-Muslim riots. There is a role of a newly-wed daughter-in-law, and Bhisham Sahni who is directing the play wants you for the part.' I was thrilled, because I was very keen to help the Party and agreed immediately. Kaifi too, had no objections and the following evening he accompanied me to Deodhar Hall, which was tucked away in a narrow lane on the left, on the way from the Chowpatty to the Opera House.

It was a small theatre where IPTA had its rehearsals every evening at six o'clock. I saw many faces light up as I walked in and was reassured by the warmth of my welcome. In those days, the Communist Party was like a large family where people were there for each other, and envy simply did not exist. Prem Dhawan's fiancée Noor was a member of IPTA and around my age, she could have resented losing the role to me, instead she continued being warm and friendly.

A whole new world opened up to me. It was here that I first met Zohra Sehgal from whom I was to learn a great deal about acting. She was playing the part of a bangle seller in the play. One day during a rehearsal I saw her rubbing her white burqah in the mud with her feet. I summoned the courage to ask what she was doing. She laughed and said, 'Have you ever seen a bangle seller in such a sparkling white burqah? I am trying to make it look weather beaten.' As our rehearsals progressed, I watched Zohraji add gestures and expressions to her character that made the bangle seller come alive. I can still hear her bursting into a cackle just like countless bangle sellers that I had heard, as she accepted a paan from Uzraji, who was playing her mother-in-law. I was captivated by the manner in which Zohraji worked to inhabit the world of the character she was playing.

The play opened in Sunderbhai Hall and was a great success. There were a few comrades, however, who thought that although my performance was very good, my voice did not carry to the back rows. I took note of their criticism and worked hard on my voice. What was most important was that my director Bhisham Sahni was pleased with my performance and decided to offer me the lead role in his new play, *Ghost Train*. This was a difficult and complicated role of a girl who appears to be very innocent but is actually a cunning British agent who supplies arms to the Hindus and weapons to the Muslims. Balraj Sahni played the role of the C.I.D. Inspector who finally arrests me. Playing this two-faced girl was a challenge and I was nervous, but Kaifi was even more anxious. He was not sure that I could do justice to the role but I was very keen on the part and worked tirelessly at perfecting it. That year the IPTA Conference was held in Ahmedabad, and *Ghost Train* was performed there before an audience of twelve thousand people to much applause and critical acclaim. I returned to the city after nearly thirty years with my daughter Shabana and was surprised to find that people there remembered my performance.

4

In Search of a Home

KAIFI'S FATHER WAS a zamindar and lived in a small village called Mijwan in District Azamgarh in Eastern U.P. His family members were simple and affectionate people who were bound by old traditions and educated their girls at home because they did not believe in sending them to school. They observed strict purdah. Before entering the house Abba, Kaifi's father, would clear his throat as a signal for all concerned to present themselves with propriety; anybody who was lying down would sit up or if a husband and wife were sitting too close to each other, they would move apart.

In 1948 when I was expecting my first child, Kaifi took me to Lucknow to meet his family. My in-laws were fairly conservative and orthodox Shi'a but they took me to their hearts, even though I was a Sunni and did not observe purdah. His elder brother Yusuf Hussain Rizvi, whom we called Achchan Bhaiyya, was a lawyer and lived in Dali Ganj, a new part of the city. He looked after all my expenses, but I lived with Wajida Baji, Kaifi's beloved older sister, who was warm and affectionate as were Achchan Bhaiya and his wife Dulhan Bhabi. Wajida Baji lived in Nakhkhas, an old part of a city steeped in traditions. From dawn to well past dusk, the streets were full of the distinct cries of vendors extolling their wares, and selling cream, fruit, yoghurt, qulfi and other delicacies.

Our friend Munish Narain Saxena who was from Lucknow happened to be there at the time. Often, he would cycle over to

Baji's house to visit us. Sometimes Kaifi would hire a tonga, and hang curtains up on all sides to form an enclosure where the two of us would sit together. With Munish cycling alongside, we would head off to Hazrat Ganj and sit in a coffee house for hours, deep in conversation dissecting the present and planning the future. One day, we gave the curtains to a laundry and headed home in an open tonga. When Baji learnt of it she merely said, 'Dulhan, in our family the absence of purdah is frowned upon.' I thought it best to keep silent.

There was no question of my visiting the chowk where the tawaif lived because women from respectable families could not afford to be seen in the locality. It was many years later when I visited Lucknow in 1975 to nurse Kaifi (who was in hospital with a broken leg) that I was able to visit the chowk. All of Kaifi's relatives had moved to Pakistan after Partition and I was free to roam the narrow alleyways. It was a world like no other – row upon row of shops lined the narrow alleyways. Some sold nihari, kulchay, tunday ke kebab and other gastronomic delights while others carried exquisite Lucknow chikan embroidery. I stepped into shops to inspect the engraved silver khasdans and pandans and stopped to look at silver leaf being pounded. I could not resist the flowers and bangles, and of course the attars, the famous perfumes of the city.

❦

On 26 April 1948, my first child was born in a hospital in Lucknow and my father-in-law named him Khayyam. Some women from a neighbouring room dropped in to see Amma, my mother-in-law and asked her, 'Chachi, has Athar had a boy or a girl?' Looking rather glum, she replied, 'A girl.' I was astonished and the moment they left I said, 'But Amma, I have had a boy!' She put her finger on her lips and said, 'Ssh...not so loud. Women here are very quick to cast an evil eye!' I was surprised at the importance given to the birth of a male child. Sixty years later, it remains a matter of collective shame that in India, female infanticide is a frequent occurrence and often the female foetus is killed before birth . As a result of this there are some areas in India where young men cannot find brides, because there simply are not enough girls in the local population.

ༀ

Four months after Khayyam was born, we went to Kaifi's village Mijwan. We travelled by train from Lucknow to Shahganj station from where we took a narrow gauge train to Phulpur, the local tehsil town. There was no road leading to Mijwan and we had to travel the last two kilometers, through open fields, in a palanquin. From the moment I set foot in the village, local women came in droves to inspect me. Even though I had been married for over a year, in their presence I had to sit demurely with my head covered and my eyes lowered. It seemed that most of them approved of me but one was overheard saying, 'Chachi's stock has been ruined!' implying that, as I was not a Shi'a but a Sunni, I had hybridized and lowered the standing of future generations of Kaifi's family. While Kaifi's house was quite large, the village was so small that it did not have a village stall where you could buy a matchbox or soap. There was no electricity and no running water. Water had to be drawn from a well, and for this job Abba had settled a Dhunia family on his land. They were named after their profession, which was to clean and prepare cotton wool to fill quilts and mattresses. Our Dhunia's wife Rahmatia, who was always most stylishly turned out and laden with silver jewellery, fetched water from the well, while her sister Tulia did the cooking.

In Mijwan, Kaifi and I lived in a simply furnished room, which had a table, a chair and two beds. Here, Khayyam and I would take our afternoon nap, while Kaifi busied himself writing poetry. We had to make do with a manual punkha suspended across the ceiling with a cord. It was made of cloth, about two feet high and eight feet wide, Kaifi would tie the cord to his toe and tug away as he wrote. He became the butt of village tomfoolery, because according to local rules no husband in his right mind would contemplate waiting upon his wife. Kaifi's friends would mimic him as they pulled imaginary punkha cords. We were in Mijwan for four long months. If Amma and Wajida Baji had not regaled me with stories of Kaifi's childhood, I could not have endured the cloistered existence inside the house for so long.

Born into a Shi'a family, Kaifi had grown up hearing members of his family, particularly Wajida Baji, recite Mir Anis's marsiyas. Baji told me that Kaifi was drawn to poetry from his childhood. When he was eight and the family was observing Nauroz, the Persian new year, he surprised everyone by reciting a couplet, in his childish lisp:

> *From all quarters of the world the breeze announced*
> *Spring is here, spring is here, spring is here.*

I asked Baji to tell me how Kaifi became a poet. 'That is a long story,' she said smiling, but I insisted and so she began, 'It was because of Abba that our home was full of poetry. We had regular mushairas in our house, at least once a month, and all my older brothers participated. As Athar was considered too young he was given the task of serving tea and paan.' Baji was an excellent raconteur and as she spoke the scenes began to move before my eyes as though on a cinema screen.

There is a hum of activity in the baithak. Athar's older brothers, Zafar Bhaiyya, Achchan Bhaiyya and Shabbir Bhaiyya are over from Lucknow. Chandni covers the floor. People begin to arrive and take their seats. Athar's father is seated, reclining against a bolster and talking to a friend. It is the setting for a mushaira.

In the inner courtyard, Baji is sitting on a takht covered with a carpet, making paan. In the kitchen, Kaifi's younger sister Shabbiri is preparing tea. Amma is busy cutting betel nut.

AMMA

(*Nervous they might run out of water*) Ai Tulia, hurry and fetch fresh water from the well; and don't forget the pitchers outside also need filling up.

Shabbir Bhaiyya is standing in one corner of the courtyard, holding a pencil and notebook in his hand. He is deep in thought and looks worried; clearly the muse has deserted him. Athar who is standing near Baji, waiting for the paan to be made, walks towards Shabbir Bhaiyya.

ATHAR

(Concerned) What's the matter Shabbir Bhaiyya?

SHABBIR BHAIYYA

Nothing you'll understand… the mushaira is about to start and I am finding it impossible to compose a ghazal on the given misra.

ATHAR

(Softly) Bhaiyya, if you permit me, I can compose the ghazal. You don't have to mention my name.

SHABBIR BHAIYYA

(Smiling and handing the notebook and pencil to Athar) Well, go ahead then. Let's see how accomplished you are. The misra-e-tarah is 'I laughed so much I could not contain my tears.'

Shortly afterwards

ATHAR

(Walks towards Shabbir Bhaiyya and recites a ghazal)

Can there be such sorrow as we live through our years

Where there's no peace in laughter, no comfort in tears?

Another heart, would torn apart

But I continue to smile and drink sorrowful tears

She looked upon me with favour after a long age

Though my heart was pleased, I could not contain my tears.

SHABBIR BHAIYYA

(In shock) What! If you have composed this ghazal you have every right to participate in the mushaira.

ATHAR

How will I get permission?

SHABBIR BHAIYYA

Come along and I shall plead your case with Abba. After all you have composed the ghazal.

Athar enters the gathering. Shabbir Bhaiyya whispers something in Abba's ear. Abba nods his head in consent. The mushaira begins.

Pleased, but reticent Athar recites the whole poem. Cries of appreciation rise in the air; but it is clear that everyone thinks he is merely reciting a ghazal composed by his older brother. Athar runs to the courtyard and on seeing Baji he bursts into tears.

ATHAR

Baji, you will see, one day I will become a great poet.

BAJI

Yes, yes, of course. Why not, if you work hard you will. For now, just take the paan outside.

Wajida Baji told me another story about Kaifi and Abba which made it clear that Abba was a disciplinarian who set great store by propriety, and did not let his children off lightly.

Another day: 4.00 p.m.

Athar has to go to his room, which is across the courtyard. He goes through the baithak, where Abba is sitting with his friend Babu Khan, whom Athar does not like. Athar walks past and does not greet Babu Khan. Abba finds this outrageous. After his guest departs, he summons Athar.

ABBA

Babu Khan was sitting here and you walked past without greeting him.

ATHAR

(Scratching his head) Abba, I did not see him.

ABBA

I understand. These things happen. Do you see those palm trees in front of you? Now go and greet each one of them in turn.

Athar was stunned, because there were a hundred and fifty trees or more. However, Abba's orders could not be ignored. Athar walked up to the trees.

ATHAR

(Crying, as he goes up to each tree) Salam, salam, salam, salam....
Abba sits drinking his tea and watching Athar, until he greets the last tree.

ABBA

(Summoning Athar) Come, now you may have some tea.

Baji laughed out loud, 'Such was Abba's training.' I was fortunate to have Wajida Baji's company, because she gave me invaluable insights into Kaifi's personality. 'There are some important things you should know about Athar,' she told me, 'Heavens can fall but he will not share his troubles with anyone nor will he ask for anything. My sisters and I had instructions from Amma that one of us should be in the kitchen to give Athar his food, because rather than helping himself he would prefer to leave the kitchen on an empty stomach. Moreover he never asked for food.' I filed these nuggets of information in a corner of my mind and for the rest of our lives together, I made sure that I put the food on to Kaifi's plate. Taking him to the doctor, and giving him his medicines, were my responsibilities.

I was moved when Wajida Baji told me, 'Kaifi has always been sensitive to poverty and injustice. Even as a child he did not wear new clothes on Eid because most children in the village could not....' Baji stopped her account because she was seized by an attack of coughing and I tried to give her some support. She had tuberculosis and suffered with great courage, but with time her condition deteriorated. Her husband came to take her back to Lucknow and Amma accompanied Baji; Abba, Kaifi, our son and I were left in Mijwan. Locked up in the house for four months, my heart became weary and I said to Kaifi, 'Let us go back to Bombay.' One day we got news that Baji had died. Abba's grief broke him and Kaifi could not contain his tears. Amma returned from Lucknow a few days later. Finally, we decided to leave Mijwan.

Kaifi had no job and did not know where to house his wife and eight-month old son. We gave the matter some thought and decided that I should stay in Lucknow at Qazi Abdul Ghaffar Sahib's house, and Kaifi should go on to Bombay, find suitable accommodation and send for me. Qazi Sahib was in Hyderabad but his wife, whom everybody called Apa, made me feel very welcome for the month that I spent with her. It was here that I met Dr. Rashid Jahan, a member of the Communist Party, who worked as a medical doctor and was an established writer of Urdu fiction. She was married to Mahmuduzzafar, and together with Sajjad Zaheer and others, they had started the Progressive Writers' Movement in 1936. Every Sunday Rashida Apa would set out for an hour, with a bag full of old clothes and shoes, distributing them amongst all the needy comrades and their families. Whatsoever fit whomsoever was passed on to that person. My chappals were worn out and as her sandals fit me perfectly she took them off and gave them to me. One day, she visited us wearing her husband's checked kurta. Kaifi, who was in Lucknow at the time, remarked, 'Rashida Apa your kurta is rather fetching.' She said, 'Why don't you take it. I can't take it off just now but I shall send it around first thing tomorrow.' Kaifi got it the following morning and in a well known photograph of his, he is wearing that very kurta.

5

Heartache and Fulfilment

Khayyam and I had been in Lucknow for a month before Kaifi asked me to join him. When I arrived in Bombay with my eight-month old son I found a world very different to the one I had left behind a year earlier. It was 1949 and the Commune had closed down. Sajjad Zaheer had vacated his house and gone to Pakistan, where he had been summoned by the Communist Party. Sardar Bhai and Sultana Apa were living in Bannay Bhai's house. Razia Apa had moved to Lucknow, where she was teaching in Karamat Hussain Muslim Girls' School and bringing up her three daughters, Najma, Mona and Nadira. B.T. Ranadive had replaced P.C. Joshi as General Secretary of the Party. The mood of the comrades had altered visibly, but I did not have the courage to ask questions.

Over time, I learnt that at the Second Party Congress, which had been held in Calcutta earlier that year, P.C. Joshi had been accused of being a reformist. It was said that as a friend of the Congress Party, he would be incapable of leading the Communist Party towards a revolution. B.T. Ranadive had prepared a report in which he argued that the time was ripe for a socialist revolution, because the masses were with the Communist Party. In complete contrast, P.C. Joshi was of the opinion that the masses were not with us and the Party needed a lot more time and groundwork to prepare for a revolution. The majority, however, supported Comrade Ranadive and Party policy changed.

This was the beginning of the decline of the Party. There were violent confrontations between the government and the Communists, and a ban was imposed on the Party. Many of its top leaders were thrown into jail and those who escaped arrest went underground. In the dead of night, Sardar Jafri who was fast asleep was hauled out of bed and taken to prison. Kaifi was underground because there was a warrant for his arrest. So far, he had not found a place for us to live. I spent two days in Bombay with Sultana Apa and other comrades and decided to leave for Hyderabad.

୧୬

I found that matters were not much brighter with my parents. Abbajan had retired; my two older brothers had migrated to Pakistan, and both my older sisters were in their own homes. My youngest brother, Nasrullah Khan and my three younger sisters, Qamar, Zafar and Iqbal were living at home. The family was in mourning for my sister Sardar, who had died of heart trouble a year earlier, and little Khayyam was a welcome diversion for them. He had a cherubic face and everyone called him Bhondu, which means innocent.

Of course, my life was ordered around my son. We had been in Hyderabad for three months when Khayyam, who was now eleven months old, developed a temperature. I had no money and as I did not want to burden my parents I took him to my old homeopathic doctor, who did not charge a fee. Khayyam was diagnosed with measles and was given some medicine but his condition did not improve. I took him back to the doctor who gave him some more medicine, but this too had no effect. I took my child to the homeopath yet again, and this time the doctor was quite sharp with me. I think he was vexed because he could not diagnose my son's ailments but even so, he did give him some medicine. When I reached home Khayyam was burning with a fever and Abbajan said, 'Betey, you should take him to an allopathic doctor.'

'No, he will kill my child.' I cried, 'I am terrified of allopathic doctors.' The truth was that I did not want to be a financial strain on my parents. Khayyam's condition became critical and Choti Apajan ran to Dr Josuria, who was Sarojini Naidu's son. He practised both homeopathic and allopathic medicine. I am told that when he examined Khayyam, Dr Josuria said, 'This child does not have more than twelve hours to live; he is in the third stage of tuberculosis.' My family kept the doctor's diagnosis from me.

We had planned to celebrate Khayyam's first birthday which fell on 26th April and I had embroidered a gorgeous karga kurta for him to wear at the party. Unfortunately, he was gripped by a fever on 15th April, in a matter of days his condition became critical. On 19th April 1949, seven days before his first birthday, Khayyam left me forever. It was the bleakest day of my life and my world was plunged into darkness.

Choti Apajan sent Kaifi a telegram and he came immediately. I was inconsolable; I could see my son in every corner of the house and would collapse to the ground where he had played. My father sobbed with me and my mother shed silent tears as they watched me holding my son's karga kurta to my eyes. Finally, I returned to Bombay with Kaifi. I did not want to add to his pain and could never bring myself to tell him that Khayyam lost his life to tuberculosis, most likely contracted from Wajida Baji. Many years later, I was told that when Khayyam's condition became critical, Bari Apajan had rushed to call the doctor but she was delayed because she had to wait for His Eminence the Nizam's motorcade to pass. When the doctor finally arrived my son had breathed his last. I cannot forgive the Nizam for this.

❧

Mahendernath and Kaifi were working like men possessed to organize the All-India Progressive Writers' Conference in Bhiwandi, a suburb of Bombay. As the ban on the Party had not been lifted, they had to make all the arrangements while underground, and were able to do so with the help of some Party workers. All the great Progressive Writers assembled at the Conference: Majaz Lucknavi,

Krishan Chandar, Ismat Chughtai, Shahid Latif, Rajinder Singh Bedi, Vishwamitra Adil, Habib Tanvir, S. M. Mehdi, Munish Narain Saxena and Sultana Jafri, (Sardar Jafri was in prison at the time). Jan Nisar Akhtar was joined by his wife Safia Apa, who brought their two little boys, Javed and Salman with them. Javed, who is also called Jadu, and must have been four or five at the time, spent the entire day jumping and climbing all over the chairs. Instead of restraining him Safia Apa looked at him indulgently. Zohra Jamal's sister Akhtar Jamal gave a rousing speech, 'Our pens should be red, our ink should be red, our stories and our poems should be red; everything we write should be red.' Majaz rose and said, tongue firmly in cheek, 'Madam, please, allow us some pink!'

It was during this conference that the new manifesto for the Progressive Writers was launched. Though the conference was a diversion, my sorrow was unbearable. I could not forget my little son and carried his kurta with me at all times. If I saw a one-year old child at a bus stop or somewhere else, my legs would give way and I would sink to the ground, weeping, and holding Khayyam's kurta to my eyes. Gradually, it became clear to me that most people feel uncomfortable around those who cannot control their grief and tend to walk away from them. I had to control my behaviour and hide my pain. In time I learnt to smile.

On my return from Hyderabad I had moved in with Sultana Apa at 7 Sikri Bhavan, but I found it difficult to accept that everything about the Party had changed. Sectarianism was rife and there was none of the old camaraderie. The comrades regarded each other with suspicion as though a spy were lurking in every corner. If coming to terms with the grief of losing my child was not enough to contend with, I had to face the incomprehensible behaviour of the comrades.

I had no knowledge of where Kaifi was and had to depend on one of the comrades to take me to him, because they were the only ones who knew where he was hiding. Sometimes, two or three weeks would pass between our meetings. I would stay the night with

Kaifi and steal out the following morning. Poor Kaifi was running around the city; he spent many nights at Rajinder Singh Bedi's, and then who knows where else. He had salutary encounters with some well-to-do people who had always professed sympathy for the Party. When he turned up at their doorsteps seeking shelter, they made feeble excuses for their inability to help him, he had to be on the run once again. On the other hand, notwithstanding her brusque ways, Ismat Apa never failed members of the Party. One night, when Kaifi arrived at her doorstep, famished and exhausted, Ismat Apa rushed into the kitchen, took out half a dozen kebabs from the fridge, fried them and made hot parathas for him. At about one o'clock in the morning, just as Kaifi had finished eating, he had to flee because somebody had tipped off the police and there was danger of his being arrested. Kaifi had grown a moustache as a disguise, and when I saw him I exclaimed, 'Goodness, you look like a police constable.' With his usual wit he responded, 'perhaps that's why I escaped arrest.'

Many comrades were homeless and several, like me, had moved into number 7 Sikri Bhavan. It was decided that each comrade should give Sultana Apa fifty rupees a month for food, but Vishwamitra Adil was the only one who did this with any regularity. Habib Tanvir, Kanwal Narain and Ahuja were there, and Dina also moved in after her release from prison. We kept a cook on a monthly salary of two hundred rupees. All of us knew when Sultana Apa was running out of money, because she would tie ten kilos of potatoes and ten kilos of onions to a rope and inform the cook that this was all we had. Thereafter, every day we would eat potatoes. There were times when we ate roti with just daal and raw onions. There was countrywide rationing and a shortage of sugar, and every comrade carried a Gold Leaf cigarette tin full of sugar to the breakfast table. Dina never carried her own tin and Habib Tanvir would give her a spoonful from his.

One day, we got news that all the comrades in jail were on hunger strike. In solidarity with them the Party decided to organize a big demonstration. Nearly a hundred thousand people assembled, including members of IPTA, labourers, writers, Party workers and many others. Balraj Sahni, his wife Toshji and Dina Pathak led the procession with a young boy from IPTA walking ahead of them. We reached Kamgar Maidan, where the police tried to stop us but we pressed ahead, chanting slogans, 'Morarji Bhai resign! Resign, resign, resign, resign!' and 'Long live the Revolution!' including many others I cannot quite recall. Suddenly, we heard gunshots; the police had opened fire on the procession. The young boy from IPTA fell to the ground and died. The police beat up Balraj Sahni, Toshji and Dina Pathak brutally; they were dragged into vans and packed off to jail. There was pandemonium. This was the first time I had participated in a procession that had been fired upon. I ran for my life. I knew I was trampling over some helpless women but I kept running. How horrid is the fear of death! I ran into a labourer's house. I was trembling like a leaf; the wife comforted me and gave me a glass of water. The husband reassured me in typical Bombay speak, 'Don't you be afraid Bai; nobody will come here looking for you. When things settle down I shall take you home. Where do you live?' Petrified, I answered, '7, Sikri Bhavan, Walkeshwar Road.' 'Alright, alright, I'll take you there.' We could hear the sound of bullets, and people screaming. Kaifi, Munish and Mehdi were searching for me, but not a soul knew where I was. At midnight, when Kaifi arrived at number 7 Sikri Bhavan he was visibly relieved to find me there.

∞

I was expecting my second child and after a long time I was happy, but the Party was not pleased. Orders were given for me to have an abortion, because as the Party argued, 'Shaukat is not earning and Kaifi is underground. Who will provide for the newborn child?' I was mortified. The Party called a meeting to discuss the matter. I stood my ground, saying, 'I want this child and I shall find the means to look after it.' All the comrades tried to prevail upon me but I had made up my mind. Our friend Mehdi was the only comrade who stood by me. Finally, the Party had no choice but to endorse my decision to have my baby. I decided that I would go home to my parents in Hyderabad and upon my return I would earn sufficient money to provide for myself and for my child.

∞

In Hyderabad my mother welcomed me with open arms and all my younger siblings who loved me dearly fussed over me and catered to my every need. This was just a few years after the debacle with the Razakars and the Communist Party had launched an appeal asking people to sign a petition in favour of the Peace Movement. Baji, Akhtar Bhai's older sister and I volunteered to take the campaign into middle class homes. One day we walked into a courtyard where two women were busy cooking and another was breastfeeding her baby. One of them asked in typical Hyderabadi, 'Where have you all come from, Ma?' Baji responded in the sweetest possible manner, 'May we sit down? We'd like to talk to you ladies.' Pointing towards me, she continued, 'This is Kaifi Azmi's wife, and my name is Jamal-un-Nisa, I teach young girls sewing and embroidery.' The woman's attitude softened immediately and she said, 'Sit, sit…' pointing to a dhurrie spread on the floor.

We sat down and Baji produced the appeal, saying, 'You must be aware of the terrible consequences of war. All of us have witnessed the conflict between the Razakars and the Indian Union. Too many young men have lost their lives and many young women have been dishonoured. That is why we think that this madness should stop.' The women began to look a trifle bored. Baji extended a piece of paper towards them and said, 'Please, do sign our appeal. It says that there should never be another war and peace should prevail forever.' The woman looked shocked at the mention of a signature and called out to her sister-in-law, 'Aji, Bhabijan, I do not know what on earth these women are talking about that "peace is good or war is good"; but they say we must sign this petition.' Bhabijan exclaimed, as she added tarka to her daal, 'Ooi, how can we women sign without asking our men folk? Tell them to go away and return tomorrow; we shall ask the men.' We left the house and once out of earshot I burst out laughing and said to Baji, 'I am afraid this is too tedious. Count me out of this one.' But Baji did not lose heart; she continued knocking on doors, asking for signatures for the appeal.

I had been in Hyderabad for five months when Ammajan decided to call Bago, the midwife, to check if my baby was in the correct position. Bago Dai could hold her own with the top gynaecologists of the time and many women in Hyderabad had more confidence in her than in qualified doctors. About fifty-five to sixty years old, she had an attractive face with a dark complexion and salt and pepper hair. She had no sight in either eye. Her lips were reddened by the cachetu from the paan that she chewed constantly, and this emphasized her perpetual broad smile. Around her neck she had an exquisite piece of gold Telangana jewellery, called 'gutta phussal'; today a good one can set you back for as much as fifteen lakh rupees, but even at the time it could not have cost less than ten to fifteen thousand rupees. In her ears she wore typical Hyderabadi gold earrings called gentiyan.

Bago arrived with her granddaughter in an auto-rickshaw, dressed in a bright sari with a contrasting border and a choli that tied into a knot at the front. I was seven months pregnant. She felt my stomach all over and pressing it hard, she said in local Deccani, 'Bibi, why d'ya go to the medicine house, the baby is absolutely fine. The kind of lady doctors they have over there, as soon as the pain starts they snuff you out with chloroform! Day before yesterday they snuffed Zahra Begum, the teacher. After the delivery when they tried to bring her around with oxygen, they couldn't find a single cylinder in the grand Osmania hospital. Poor thing, without ever setting eyes on her newborn son, she is sitting at God's right hand.' I almost died of fright. In any case I was terrified of hospitals, and exclaimed, 'Bago, you had better be there!' Ammajan handed her a paan and asked, 'I hope there is nothing to worry about?'

'O no, Pasha' Bago reassured her. 'Now why on earth should I lie? By the grace of Bhagwan, all will be well. There is a long time to go. Manjhle Pasha knows my house. Just send for me and before you know it, I shall be with you.' In Hyderabad, Pasha is a term of respect used for older ladies, and this was how Bago Dai addressed Bari Apajan.

On the night of 17 September 1950 when my pains started, Ammajan immediately sent for Bago. True to her word she was there within half an hour, and as usual accompanied by her granddaughter. At a quarter to three, on the morning of 18 September, Madam Shabana arrived. Ammajan, Kaifi, Choti Apajan and my other siblings were there. Ammajan put the baby on the scales used for weighing rice and grain: at seven and three quarter pounds she was a healthy and pretty baby. Bago washed and bathed her, wrapped her in a cloth and handed her to me. I saw a pretty little girl with a small pink mouth, a head of thick black hair and a healthy fair complexion, and my eyes brimmed over with tears. Ammajan gave Bago some money and a sari.

Kaifi had to get back to Bombay. Ismat Apa and her husband, Shahid Latif were making films, and had commissioned him to write two songs. They sent me a thousand rupees. Throughout my pregnancy Ismat Apa had been very kind to me. Occasionally, she would take me to her home and ensure I got some rest. There were times when she paid for my medicines. I discovered that the real Ismat Apa was warm and caring, quite unlike the brusque and caustic image she projected.

ॐ

When Shabana was four months old Kaifi took me back to Bombay. By now the ban on the party had been lifted, but Kaifi still had trouble finding a home for us, because while I was able to compromise on almost everything else, I had one condition: I was not willing to cook in the room I was going to live in. Finally, Kaifi's friend Masood Siddiqui found us two rooms on the fourth floor of a tenement on Dimtimkar Road. It was a chawl, and as the previous owner had not paid his bill, the electric supply had been cut off. The walls were smeared with dead bedbugs and stained with paan spittle. I got hold of a brush and scrubbed the door, walls and floor. As was my practice, I cut up an old sari to make curtains and hung them on the windows. The toilet was shared and even today, sixty years later, thinking of the stench makes my stomach churn.

Not long after we had moved, I had to go to Nagpur on tour with IPTA, where I found some curtains and bedcovers for our room for just fifteen rupees each. I often went for walks with Munish who knew all the secret shortcuts in the city. I would get Oleander flowers from the Hanging Gardens and arrange them in a brass vase. Finally, life in those rooms grew bearable.

It was while we were living in the chawl that Ammajan, Choti Apajan and Akhtar Bhai came to stay with us in Bombay. This was the first time they were visiting us. It was a particularly hot summer, and as the electricity had been disconnected the fan could not be used. For light we used a kerosene lantern and a dibri, which created a powerful stench. My visitors were so uncomfortable that they chose to spend the night sitting at the Chowpatty beach. The following morning they decided to return to Hyderabad. I was not particularly embarrassed, as I did not find my life difficult: in India millions of people were living far worse lives. Ammajan was very pained by what she saw and though she did not say anything she left five hundred rupees under my pillow. I had never asked my parents for money, nor did I lament the fact that Kaifi and I were hard up.

By the time we found these rooms I had started working for Prithvi Theatre where my salary was a hundred rupees a month. I earned an additional forty-five rupees from a boy who came for tuition to our rooms at five o'clock in the evening. Kaifi was working regularly in an area called Madanpura, where he spent most of his time amongst the labourers. He continued to write his poetry, lying on a loose stringed charpoy. It was here that he wrote his poem *Makaan* (House), which became very famous and was used by Shahid Latif in his film *Sone ki Chidiya* (The Golden Bird) in 1958.

House

A scorching wind blows tonight,
Sleep will not come on the footpath tonight
Wake up everyone, I too shall wake up, you too must wake up
A window will open in this wall tonight
The earth was ready to devour us, even as
We descended from broken branches
Neither these houses nor the dwellers inside know
Of the days we spent in caves

Our hands moulded new forms and we did not tire
When we embellished our creations
We built the walls higher and higher
As we decorated doorways and arches

Storms had extinguished the flames of our lamps
We lit the darkness with electric stars
Once the house was built, a stranger was hired to watch over it
And we slept on the ground, surrounded by the din of
*   construction*
With the fatigue of a hard day's labour in every fibre of our
*   being*
With the image of the new home in our eyes
This is how the day melts on our heads;
And night pierces our eyes like black arrows.

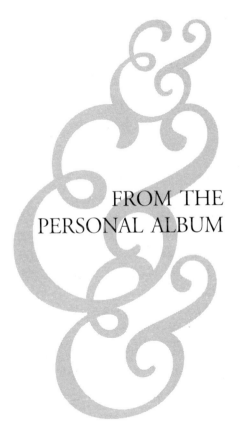

FROM THE
PERSONAL ALBUM

Yahya Khan, Abbajan,
Shaukat's progressive father,
a man ahead of his times

Made for each other –
the young, romantic Kaifi (top)
and a radiant, lovely Shaukat
(right)

At the Progressive Writers
Association conference in
Hyderabad (1947). From
left, Majrooh Sultanpuri,
Sardar Jafri, Kaifi signing
an autograph book, Ismat
Chughtai in dark glasses and
behind her Riasat Khanam

Kaifi and Shaukat with their
first-born, Khayyam

TOP: Celebrating Holi with colleagues from Prithvi Theatre. Standing at back, Prithvi Theatre's manager, Nandji; second row, from left, Shaukat, Kumud Lele with Zohra Sehgal's son, Pavan, in her lap, front row from left Razia Sachdev, Indumati Lele

TOP RIGHT: A tranquil moment – sipping nariyal pani at Juhu beach

BOTTOM RIGHT: At their 25th wedding anniversary with son Baba and daughter Shabana, 23 May 1972

PREVIOUS PAGE: Happy together – Shaukat and Kaifi

TOP: Kaifi, Shabana and Shaukat

BOTTOM: A delighted mother, Shaukat with Shabana and Javed on their wedding day, 9 December 1984

TOP: The family. From left,
Tanvi, Shaukat, Kaifi, Shabana.
Seated at back, Baba and right,
Javed

BOTTOM: Mother and daughter
in a playful mood, at
Shabana's 50th birthday,
18 September 2000

TOP: In her own right –
Shaukat at the foundation
ceremony of the school in
Mijwan

BOTTOM: Baba and Shabana
bonding together in Janki
Kutir, 1989

TOP: The three sisters. From left, Liaqat Khanam, Shaukat Kaifi and Riasat Khanam

BOTTOM: Lata Mangeshkar and Gulzar with Kaifi Azmi and Shaukat Kaifi

"Rasgulla Baba" and "Dulhan
Pasha" Tanvi

AN ACTOR
PREPARES

LEFT: As *Pagli* in the play of the same name, for Sajjan's Triveni Rang Manch. She won the best actress award for this performance in the Maharashtra State Drama Competition

TOP: With Ram Singh in her most applauded role for IPTA's *Afrika Jawan Pareshan*

TOP: As Amma, grieving at the death of her daughter in M S Sathyu's *Garm Hawa*, 1973

RIGHT: As one of Ranjha's bhabis in Chetan Anand's *Heer Ranjha*, 1970

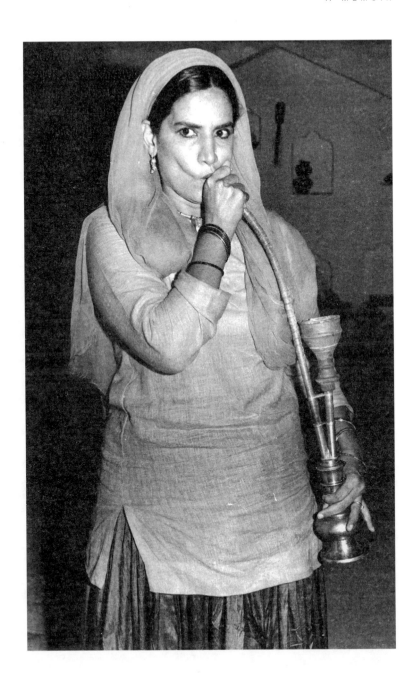

PREVIOUS PAGE: As the madam of the brothel with Nana Patekar in Mira Nair's *Salaam Bombay*, 1998

in *Umrao Jaan* 1982 (top) and the old fixer Chuhiya Begum in *Anjuman* 1985 (bottom) both directed by Muzaffar Ali

LEFT: A study in contrasts – as the glamorous Khanam Jaan

TOP: A picture of domesticity, with Balraj Sahni in *Garm Hawa*

At her dramatic best at IPTA's
50th anniversary

6

Red Flag Hall

After six months in Dimtimkar Road, we finally managed to get a room, through Sardar Bhai and Munish's efforts, in the building where they lived. Red Flag Hall was a large flat in Arab Building at Prarthana Samaj. The flat was controlled by the Party and the drawing room was used for its meetings. There were eight other rooms and each room was home to a comrade and his family, for which they paid a rent of fifty rupees a month, which would not pay for a dozen eggs today. Prarthana Samaj is a ten minute walk from the Opera House and was therefore very convenient for me to get to rehearsals which began at nine o'clock every morning and finished at two o'clock in the afternoon.

Our new room was much cleaner than our previous home but there was a problem because unlike other rooms in the flat, ours did not have a balcony. This meant that I had to cook in the room in which I lived. I told Kaifi quite plainly, that I was not willing to accept this under any circumstances. Sardar Bhai happened to hear our exchange and said, 'Moti, you can cook in the gallery behind our room.' I was touched; at least somebody cared about the way I felt. Happily, I accepted his offer, but this arrangement was not without its pitfalls. My kitchen was the passage for the sweeper woman to get to the bathroom, and she would pass behind me with her bucket and jharu while I was cooking. I found this most unpleasant. Luckily, a room with a balcony soon became vacant because the Comrade who occupied it had moved to some other city. Munish, who was still single and lived on his own, said to me, 'Moti, I shall move into your room and you can take mine; it's a bit larger.' I thanked Munish profusely and accepted his offer with alacrity. As I ferried all our belongings into his room I felt I had won the lottery.

I set about adapting the room to the needs of my family. In the balcony, along one wall I kept my stove and cooking utensils and along the opposite wall, which was closer to the door that led to our room, I kept a small dining table with four chairs that I had picked up from the Chor Bazar at a monthly installment of ten rupees. I paid seventy-five rupees for the table, and a paltry fifteen for each chair. I got a carpenter to put up a bamboo screen between the cooking area and the dining table, and trained a money plant to climb over it. Now I had a proper partition between my kitchen and dining room.

When on tour with Prithvi Theatre, I would bring back gorgeous handloom textiles from different parts of India and use them as tablecloths, curtains and bedcovers. Kaifi and I had two large beds and at my favourite haunt, the Chor Bazar, I found a small one for one-year old Shabana. Not much later, I bought a cupboard for a hundred and ten rupees. My next find was a desk and chair for Kaifi. I had two steel trunks for my linen, and with an old mattress and some textiles I converted them into a sofa for our guests. In one corner of the room I fixed a winnowing fan from Uttar Pradesh and used it as a shelf for our family photographs. I have always hand stitched my sari blouses, and invariably have a collection of odd remnants of cloth lying around. In my spare time I stitched these together to make a patchwork quilt, which I hung on the wall behind our beds. Our home was finally ready for us and Kaifi was most pleased. My room was the most stylish in the commune and visitors would always ask whose room it was. Kaifi and I spent nine years in this room with our children.

I had a surfeit of luck because I now found an excellent ayah called Alice, which meant that I no longer had to drag Shabana to work every day. I would set off for the Opera House in the morning at around eight thirty or quarter to nine. Usually, I took a short cut around the back of the police station, a route closed to cars and other vehicles and therefore safe for pedestrians. Every morning, I saw a woman in her mid-thirties filling buckets with water from the municipal tap and washing the taxis that were parked there. The woman had two sons and a daughter; the boys were aged around eight and six, while the girl must have been about five years old. Sometimes, I would see her standing in front of a shop, combing her daughter's hair as she was getting her ready for school. The floor of the shop was raised from the ground and rested on four stilts some two feet above the ground. The woman's cooking stove was kept under the floor; perhaps the shopkeeper had given the place to her out of the goodness of his heart. Her husband was a good-for-nothing. Invariably he was asleep but occasionally I saw him washing a taxi.

This woman made a lasting impression on me. Whenever I had a moment to spare I would stop and chat with her. Her name was Kamla Bai; she was from some village near Madras and had come to Bombay in search of employment. She always wore clean clothes and appeared to be busy and cheerful, even though there were times when her husband would disappear for two to three months. When I enquired after him she would tell me in Bombay Hindi, 'Arrey Bai, I can't rely on him. When it takes his fancy he goes off to the village and when it suits him he comes back. I don't want to live in the village because there is no school there. The cost of living is not so high these days and I can afford the children's school fees, besides my children are learning English. I want to educate them so they can make something of their lives. It is impossible to find a home in this city but people here have been very good to me and have given me a place to live.'

'What do you do during the monsoon?' I asked out of concern.

'During the rains we live under the shop. Some water does rush in from the front, but I put up plastic sheets to deal with that. In winter, too, all of us sleep under the shop, and during the summer months we sleep on the pavement. The people here are really very good and helpful.' It seems unbelievable, but that little space outside the shop was Kamla Bai's home; it was here that she tended her children when they fell ill, and it was here that she delivered her fourth baby, with the help of a local midwife, behind a temporary curtain. In all the years that I knew her Kamla Bai never asked me for money, and if I offered to give her some, she refused resolutely. I developed a profound respect for her.

Kaifi had started a Young Writers' Association for struggling authors around the time we moved into Red Flag Hall. Every Sunday they would gather at Red Flag Hall and read their stories. Sagar Sarhadi, Gulzar, Lajpat Rai and Zafar Gorakhpuri were among the many youngsters who met there. I took Sagar Sarhadi along to meet Kamla Bai. Her life had a profound impact on him and inspired him to write a one-act play called *Bhooke Bhajan Na Hoye Gopala* (The Hungry Don't Sing Songs of Praise.) Originally directed by Ramesh Talwar for IPTA, it was later performed several times in inter-collegiate competitions.

Years later, after we had moved to Juhu and both my children were successful adults in their own fields, I went to buy Kolhapuri chappals from the area where Kamala Bai used to live. On impulse, I decided to buy some vegetables and went to the market, where I spotted a grey haired Kamala Bai. 'What are you doing here? Where are your children and your husband?' I bombarded her with questions. She smiled and said, 'All my children are holding high positions now, and they live in flats. I live with them, but sometimes I long for this place as I have spent a lifetime here. I feel these are my people.' There was a quiet dignity about Kamla Bai that impressed all those who came in contact with her. Shabana, who had met her with me a number of times, says that her awareness of the problems faced by street dwellers and the homeless is probably rooted in her meetings with Kamala Bai.

❧

Red Flag Hall was a community of people who belonged to different parts of India and had distinct identities—rather like a bouquet of various kinds of flowers with each flower retaining its individual character. Maniben and Ambu Bhai were from Gujarat; Sawant and Shashi from Maharashtra, Sardar Jafri, Sultana Apa, Sardar Jafri's two sisters and Kaifi were from Uttar Pradesh; Sudhir Joshi and Shobha Bhabi were from Madhya Pradesh and I was from Hyderabad. Each family lived in a single room and all of us had converted our balconies into kitchens. Between us we shared one bathroom and one toilet, but in the nine years that I lived in Red Flag Hall, I never witnessed any disagreement or quarrel over these facilities, which were kept clean at all times. All of us joined together to celebrate Holi, Diwali and Eid. Each family had at least one child and some even two. The children may have had disagreements or fights amongst themselves but no mother ever came complaining to another. Sultana Apa was called 'Amma' by all the children and Sardar Jafri, was 'Doda'. I was 'Mummy' for all, Kaifi was 'Abba' and Shobha Bhabi was 'Bhabi'.

As my children grew older and started school, I could not take them on tour with Prithvi Theatre and left them with Alice. I never had to worry that the children would take my absence to heart and develop complexes. Shabana and Baba were happy children. All the children in Red Flag Hall played together and in times of trouble or illness all the mothers got together to look after them. All the men were Party members but of the women, only Sultana Apa was. We all came from different religious backgrounds but we shared a worldview: the love of humanity.

In the fifty-five years that I was married to Kaifi I met some remarkable people. I take great pride in the fact that I had the opportunity of being close to Sardar Jafri. In Red Flag Hall our room was opposite his, and over a decade I witnessed many acts that were a testament to his compassion and love for his wife, children and sisters. He spent most of his time reading and writing at his desk in his one-room home. It was from here that he made his extraordinary contributions to Urdu literature. It was from here that he travelled to Russia and came back laden with gifts for all of us. Sardar Bhai knew of my abiding weakness for tea cosies and I remember well that from one of his trips he brought for me a quaint doll wearing a flared frock, which really was a tea cosy unlike any that I had seen. Even though I was living in one room, my tea set was always of the finest bone china. I served tea off a smart tray cloth and there was always a cosy for the teapot. Sardar Bhai's doll cosy added an unusual dimension to my tea service.

It was part of my daily routine to return home from Prithvi Theatre at two o'clock, have lunch, and take a nap. Sometimes, I would wake up to find Sardar Bhai at Kaifi's desk rummaging through his papers. I would ask, 'Sardar Bhai, what are you looking for?' He would respond with a smile, 'Kaifi has a very cavalier attitude towards his poems. He will scribble something profound on a cigarette box, on a matchbox or any random piece of paper. I am trying to retrieve whatever I can, before it finds its way into the dustbin.'

After his parents died, Sardar Bhai asked his sisters to move from Balrampur to live with him. Sitara and Rabab were intelligent and independent young women, who became good friends of mine. In Bombay, they enrolled in a night school from where they completed their matriculation. Rabab, whom I called Rabbo Baji, worked in Madanpura where she had saris embroidered, and sold them to stars like Lata Mangeshkar and Naseem Bano. Sitara worked in Dr Ghosh's naturopathy clinic, helping out with his patients. In this way, they were able to make a contribution to the running of the household. One day, there was no money in our house and consequently nothing was cooked. Rabbo Baji told Sardar Bhai, 'I don't think Shaukat has had anything to eat.' Immediately, he asked Rabbo Baji to fetch me. I was moved to tears but did not go, saying that I had eaten. That evening Sardar Bhai came into my room and quietly left a hundred rupees on Kaifi's desk.

When Shabana was three years old, Sultana Apa, an Inspector of children's schools at the time, arranged for her to be admitted to the local Municipal school. Her sons Pappu and Chunnam, who were actually called Nazim and Hikmat after the Turkish poet, were at the same school. It was an ordeal to get Shabana to the school bus. Such was the little toddler's loathing for the school that she would jump out of the ayah's arms and sit on the road, kicking her heels as the ayah tried to drag her off, unsuccessfully. Two people would have to lift Shabana and carry her into the bus. When her school report arrived I froze: in every subject she had attained, 'Nought! Nought! And… Nought!' Horrified, I told Sultana Apa, 'I am not sending my child to this school, she is not a duffer, she is protesting.' Sultana Apa withdrew all three children from the school. Quite unexpectedly, Kaifi announced, 'I am going to send my daughter to Queen Mary's High School.'

I cried out, 'Arrey, I can't believe this! The fees for this school are thirty rupees a month. How are we going to pay so much?'

Kaifi responded quite firmly, 'Don't you worry; I shall earn the money for my daughter's education.' There was, however, another insurmountable obstacle. Queen Mary's had a requirement that both parents should know English which neither Kaifi nor I did. We found a way out: Sultana Jafri and Munish Narain Saxena went as Shabana's parents. It was here that Shabana's correct upbringing began and for this as for so many other things I shall remain indebted to Sultana Apa. I was amazed to see little Shabana metamorphose into a completely different child and all her school reports after that were excellent. It was at this school that she developed an interest in acting. Ever the perfectionist, Shabana was ten years old when she took her Abba's silk kurta on the quiet, to wear as a toga for her role as Mark Anthony in Shakespeare's *Julius Caesar.* She was cast in every school play thereafter.

When I was expecting my son Baba, Sultana Apa had me registered at St. George's Hospital where I did not have to pay for pre-natal examinations because it was run by the Government. However, when I went into labour Kaifi had to borrow five rupees from the paan shop opposite our home for the taxi to take me to the hospital. On September 13, 1953 my son was born. When I saw him I felt that everything in the world had fallen into place. He weighed eight pounds and was a sweet and healthy baby, with a head full of thick black hair, beautiful big eyes and a distinct nose. The following day Kaifi came to see his son with his friend Munish and on the fifth day I was discharged. Shabana, who was now three and was waiting for us with Alice in a taxi, looked at me with amazement when I showed her a little bundle wrapped up in cloth and told her that this was her brother. She was amused and insisted that I put the baby on her lap, when thankfully, we arrived home and Alice took Baba from me. I went upstairs to our room and wept uncontrollably because I felt that God had sent my Khayyam back to me. Everyone gathered around the baby and Sultana Apa said, 'He looks exactly like Kaifi.'

Kaifi was working in Madanpura as a Party whole-timer but he was constantly looking for paid work to supplement our income. Sometimes he wrote songs for producers like Nanubhai Vakil or a screenplay for Lekhraj Bhakri. He earned five thousand rupees for a film, which included writing the screenplay and the songs. This was sufficient for our family for a few months. Shabana's fees and Alice's salary were paid from this money. I had stopped working just before Baba was born but when he was two months old I resumed work with Prithvi Theatre.

Kaifi had been writing film lyrics for some years when he was asked to write the songs for Guru Dutt's film *Kaagaz ke Phool* (1959). A spate of big films followed, such as Mohan Gopal's *Apna Haath Jaganaath* (1960); Ramesh Sehgal's *Shola aur Shabnam* and Raj Rishi's *Ek ke Bad Ek* (1960). Unfortunately, all these films flopped even though Kaifi's songs became hits and remain popular to this day. Consequently, Kaifi was considered unlucky and he stopped getting work. It was heartbreaking for me to stand by and watch the cruel film industry cast aside someone who had written immortal lyrics like *Waqt ne kiya kya hasin sitam* (What sweet irony did time bring); and *Janay kya dhundti rahti hain yeh ankhen mujh mein?* (Who knows what these eyes are seeking in me?)

At about eight o'clock one evening in 1963, the film maker Chetan Anand turned up quite unexpectedly at our house and said, 'Kaifi Sahib, I want you to write the songs for my next film.'

Kaifi said, 'Chetan Sahib, why court disaster? People say that my songs are not bad but my stars are unlucky.'

Chetan Anand said, 'So are mine Kaifi Sahib. Many of my films have flopped as well. You never know, minus and minus may well produce a plus.' And this is exactly what happened. The film *Haqeeqat* (1964) was a sensational hit, as were the songs. One of its songs acquired the status of an anthem.

> *Kar chale ham fida jan-o-tan sathiyon*
> *Ab tumhare havale vatan sathiyon*
>
> We have sacrificed our lives and our souls, comrades,
> Now the country is in your custody comrades

Once again in the eyes of the industry Chetan Sahib and Kaifi were stars. Kaifi would always remind us that, 'In this world of trade, relationships alter with success and failure.' But for now, Chetan Anand, the composer Madan Mohan and the lyricist Kaifi Azmi were an 'A' team. In 1970, Chetan Anand asked Kaifi to write the script for his film *Heer Ranjha* in verse; the first of its kind for Indian cinema. Kaifi worked long hours and came up with a masterpiece, which was a critically acclaimed box-office hit with many memorable songs. Kaifi's fame spread and he was inundated with offers to write lyrics. Kaifi was finally earning some decent money and a South Indian production called *Rivaaj* enabled him to buy our first car, an Ambassador on instalments. One afternoon he was sitting in front while I was sitting in the back with my friend Razia, when Kaifi turned around happily and said, 'I say, now you are a lady with a car!' I could not resist putting on airs.

7

Treading the Boards

In 1951 Zohra Sehgal introduced me to Prithvi Theatre. One Sunday morning she took me to see their production of *Pathan* at the Opera House, which was home to the Company.

As the play started I was transported to a street in Peshawar:

Dawn is breaking and the Muslim call to prayer is heard as an occasional firefly glows in the fading night. A young fourteen to fifteen-year-old girl enters from the wings with a pitcher tucked under her arm; she is humming a Pushto song and has a soft smile on her face. From across the stage a young man sees the girl and climbs on to a small mound. Dressed as a Pathan, with a round turban on his head, he is Sardar of the jirga. He approaches a big gate and pushes it with his foot.

PRITHVIRAJ KAPOOR/PATHAN

(To the girl) Send for the carpenter and have this repaired.

I was riveted by the stark realism of the stage and by Prithviraj Kapoor's performance. As soon as the curtain came down I told Zohraji that I wanted to meet Papaji, as he was called by members of his company. Zohraji had already informed Prithvirajji that I would be there and he walked directly towards me the moment he spotted us. I was overawed and stood up for him. He gave me a warm smile and said, 'You will be fined one anna.'

'Why?' I asked perplexed.

'Anyone who stands up for me is penalized.' I sat down, feeling completely at ease, and told him that I would like to work with Prithvi Theatre. He looked pleased but said, 'My Workers' Fund from which members of my company can borrow money is richer than me. I shall not be able to pay you a large salary but you can certainly work with me.'

Papaji ran Prithvi Theatre with meagre funds. The company made a profit on tour, but in Bombay it ran at a loss because not many people go to the theatre on a Sunday morning. After a three-hour show, Prithvirajji would stand at the door waiting for members of the audience to make a contribution as they were leaving the theatre. The money collected went to the Theatre's Workers' Fund and was given to needy artists as a loan. In my years with Prithvi Theatre, I was a beneficiary of this facility many times.

When I joined Prithvi Theatre Kaifi and I were living in the rooms on Dimtimkar Road. Every morning at nine o'clock I would put four month old Shabana's milk bottle and clothes in my bag, strap her to my back and take the bus to the Opera House. Papaji never objected when she made gurgling noises or started crying during rehearsals. He was most accommodating, even when I would hang my little girl's clothes out to dry in the green room. My colleagues, especially Rani Azad, would keep Shabana entertained when I was on stage. Prithvi activities would wind up at two o'clock in the afternoon. As the Opera House transformed into a movie theatre, I would head home to do the cooking. Often, I would have just ten paisa in my bag, and would get palpitations thinking, 'What if my last coin is counterfeit? I will be asked to get off the bus and be humiliated in the presence of other passengers.' A few months later, after we moved to Red Flag Hall, I was spared this daily torture because it took me barely ten minutes to walk to the Opera House.

When I began work at Prithvi my salary was a hundred rupees a month and when I left six years later, I was earning two hundred and fifty rupees a month. With a regular income I was able to pay Alice, the wonderful ayah who looked after Shabana better than I could have done. Till she was three years old I would always take Shabana with me on tour and Alice came along to look after her. I was working at Prithvi when Baba was born, but Alice was so reliable and capable that I was able to go back to work after two months. Often, I took both children and Alice with me on tour. To this day I marvel at Papaji's sensitivity to the needs of working mothers. He never made me feel that my children were a burden. In fact, so many years ago he had provided us with a crèche of sorts.

Prithvirajji was a sensitive and dignified man whose attitude towards his artists was not unlike that of a father or an older brother. He had lost his mother when he was four years old and was brought up by his paternal grandfather, craving a mother's love. He was a great raconteur and often related stories from his childhood, 'When I was a little boy, after school, instead of going home I would go to a friend's house, stand at the door and watch longingly as his mother would greet him, hug him, take his bag and serve him piping hot food.' Even today this story has the power to move me. I think it was the maternal void that caused this little boy to grow up into a human being who had the gift of love.

Papaji was passionate about the theatre even as a child. He recalled, 'Once, when I was about six years old in Peshawar, I had gone with my father to see *Nal Damyanti*. In one scene the mother lifted her dead child from the ground on to her lap and started singing in a mournful voice. As the song finished the hall resounded with cries of "Encore, once more, once more." The woman put the child back on the ground, sang the song and re-enacted the whole scene! Young as I was, I knew this was wrong because it broke all illusion of reality; she should not have sung the song again. Perhaps, this experience was responsible for the birth of Prithvi Theatre, which moved away quite deliberately from the influence of the Parsi theatre towards greater realism. Papaji practised the Stanislavski method of acting. Time and again, he would explain to us, 'You should inhabit your character so completely that if your heart is ripped open it should be found beating like that of the character you are portraying.' Whether it was the Muslim setting of *Ghaddaar* or the Punjabi setting of *Ahuti*, Prithviraj Kapoor paid attention to the minutest detail of the set design and costume. Uzraji, who played the heroine opposite Prithvirajji, shared his aesthetic sensibility and designed the costumes and the sets. A father and son team, who had worked in the art department of Parsi plays, made the sets and provided the props under her direction. Zohraji, who had worked with Uday Shankar and had taught dance in his school at Almora, was the choreographer and dance instructor at Prithvi.

Papaji expected complete commitment and professionalism from us. He used every opportunity to encourage, in members of his company, a finer understanding of theatre and its relationship with culture and society. He organized special workshops on important aspects of theatre. The famous Hindi scholar Sriram Shastri who was also a very fine actor would read from the *Natyashastra* on stage. At other times we had voice training, when Papaji would make us sing to musical accompaniment, 'Allah hu, Allah hu' to the lower pitches and 'Ram, Ram' to the higher pitches.

Prithvi Theatre performances started at 9 a.m. on Sunday mornings. Papaji's idea was to transport members of the company and the audience away from the mundane into the sanctified world of theatre where a magical experience awaited them. Before the show began there was darkness all around. The sound of the shehnai and the smell of incense combined to enhance the devotional atmosphere. The musicians playing in the darkness looked like characters from Hindu mythology or the Arabian Nights. Sometimes, a shaft of light, accompanying the whispers and soft laughter of young girls from their make-up room, penetrated the darkness, enhancing the dramatic effect. Before a performance all the members of the company would assemble behind the curtain and in one voice, chant from the *Natyashastra*, 'Namame vishwa natika' in praise of the theatre. By the time the curtain rose, the actors would be totally immersed in their characters, ready to transport the audience to the world they would create on the stage.

Prithvirajji believed that art should be used to bring about social change, and his plays were not merely for entertainment but were contemporary parables. In fifteen years, Prithvi Theatre produced eight plays: *Shakuntala, Deewar, Pathan, Ghaddaar, Ahuti, Kalakaar, Paisa* and *Kisan.* While *Shakuntala* was based on Kalidasa's Sanskrit classic, all the other plays dealt with contemporary social evils. *Deewaar* was against the partition of India; *Pathan* was about Hindu-Muslim amity, and I have yet to see a better play on the subject of friendship between members of the two faiths. After watching *Pathan,* the Russian director Fedavakin embraced Papaji and congratulated him on the marvelous production. *Ahuti* depicted Hindu-Muslim hatred and how the Partition had affected the lives of ordinary people, and *Ghaddaar* explored this theme further. Both *Ahuti* and *Ghaddaar* question the creation of Pakistan as a separate country for the Muslims of India.

During a tour of south India, when we reached Cochin some members of the Muslim League raised slogans against *Ghaddaar* and threatened to burn the theatre down. Not one to be cowed down, Prithvirajji asked to meet their representatives. He invited them to watch the play, adding, 'Please reserve your judgement till you have watched the play.' The members of the Muslim League watched the play and realized that their fears were unfounded. They embraced Prithvirajji and congratulated him. Today efforts are being made to cultivate friendship between India and Pakistan, but years ago Prithvirajji understood how important it is for neighbours to live in peace. *Kalakaar* is a poignant play that explores how the innocence of the village is destroyed when it comes into contact with the city. *Kisan* is the tragic story of a small farmer whose land is taken away from him forcibly, as a result of which his wife goes mad. *Paisa* demonstrates how the love of money can bring a person to ruin. I have noticed that most artistes pay scant attention to documenting their work. Sadly, the Prithvi plays were never published. There was no video technology at the time, and the Company could not afford to have the plays filmed, these milestones of theatre are lost forever.

I toured the length and breadth of India with Prithvi Theatre, usually by train but occasionally by bus. It was not easy for the tour manager to find a place that could accommodate a hundred people. We took our bedding with us and slept on the floor. Men and women were segregated in different rooms, and though Papaji had his own room, he too slept on the floor. Invariably, the organizers would come up to him and say, 'Papaji, you on the floor! Please allow us to arrange a bed for you.' And typically, he would answer, 'Thank you. If you can provide ninety-nine beds, do bring along the hundredth for me.'

After a performance, Uzraji and he would retire to bath and change before they joined the Company for lunch, which was usually around two o'clock in the afternoon. Nothing special was ever cooked for Papaji because he ate what we ate and he ate with us. Food was cooked in large pots and served in simple stainless steel thalis. A dhurrie was spread on the floor for us to sit on. The man who served the food had instructions to let everyone have their fill. Piping hot rotis were served as members of the Company called out, 'Hey, Ram Singh, make my roti a bit crisp!' or 'I want mine fluffy.' The boy who ran to and fro serving everyone was told off routinely, 'Silly boy, is this a roti! Take it back.' Spoilt as we were, we never thought twice before sending back a runny egg and ordering a fresh one. Instead of ticking us off, Papaji would ask quietly that the discarded egg be served to him. Occasionally, when our artists returned from their shopping sprees they did not pay the rickshaw wallah but invited him to join us for a meal. Nobody questioned why this stranger was being fed—Prithvirajji's table was open to all.

I had many opportunities to witness Papaji's compassion and generosity. Once when we were in Calcutta, a stagehand called Dhondu was diagnosed with cholera. Papaji was out and nobody was willing to enter the sick man's room, which was reeking of his vomit. When Papaji returned, he ran to the sick room, ignoring the nauseous squalor and unmindful of the risk of infection, he drew Dhondu to his chest in a tight embrace. When the Doctor arrived he said, 'Prithvirajji, you have saved this young man's life by transferring the heat of your own body to his.' My respect for Papaji increased a hundredfold.

I recall another incident when we were travelling to Kashmir in three busloads. Quite suddenly, our bus came to a halt due to a roadblock on a winding mountain road. A labourer had fallen off a precipice and was badly injured. Papaji lost no time; he asked some of us to vacate our seats and got off the bus. He returned a few minutes later carrying a bleeding man with the help of two young men from the company. The injured man was made comfortable on our seats and the homeopathic doctor, who always travelled with us, dressed his wounds and gave him some medicine; but the man did not gain consciousness. Papaji took another labourer on board and gave orders for the bus to turn back and we headed for the nearest hospital. We did not continue with our journey until Papaji had ensured that the labourer would receive proper medical attention, for which he left money with his companion.

Once when Shabana was three years old, we were performing in Patna and had gone to the Buddhist sites in Gaya. On the way back, the bus had covered about ten miles when Prithvirajji asked, 'Where is Shabana?' I was sitting at the back of the bus and was under the impression Shabana was with Alice who was sitting near the front. I darted up to her shouting, 'Where is Shabana?' Alice who was looking after two-month old Baba thought Shabana was with me, and stuttered, '...but I thought Munni Baby was with you.' I felt the ground give way beneath my feet and burst into tears. Prithvirajji ordered the driver to turn back. When we reached the temple my little girl was standing alone under a large tree with tears streaming down her face. I can never forget Shabana's terrified expression, just as I shall always remember Papaji's composure and generosity.

Continuous touring for months on end had taken its toll on members of the company, and those with families were particularly fatigued. Papaji was well aware of this and in 1957 he decided to make a film based on the play *Paisa*. When the film went into production I bade farewell to the Company. My time with Prithvi

Theatres had been most rewarding, although for six years I had remained an understudy for all the roles of 'daughter' and 'wife' and did not get a chance to perform on stage. I think this might have dampened my enthusiasm at the time. When I look back, however, I can see that whatever I know about acting and theatre I learnt from Prithviraj Kapoor and Zohra Sehgal: and they continue to provide my reference points for acting. My first appearance on stage, after leaving Prithvi, was a polished performance which reflected long years of training.

Today, if I value the power of theatre it is solely because of my time at Prithvi Theatre. In the 1950s there were plenty of people who looked down upon theatre in general, and in particular on the women who worked in it. I would say to them, 'I can do what you do in your homes but can you stand on stage and deliver long dialogue? I can, and therefore I am superior to you. So, don't look upon theatre with distaste but learn to respect it.' Even today, after more than fifty years when I look back on my time at Prithvi Theatre I feel a warm glow in my heart.

One day my friend Nimmo, who was Zul Vellani's wife came to me and said, 'Amin Sayani is directing a one-act play called, *Naukarani ki Talash* (Search for a Maid) and wants you for the lead.' I accepted and the play was well received. In the audience was a man who was born Aleeq but the world knows him as Alyque Padamsee. He was the Director of a very well established company called Theatre Group, which produced English dramas. Alyque was impressed by my work and decided to direct me in an Urdu translation of Tennessee William's play *The Glass Menagerie*, translated by his friend Riffat Shamim as *Sheeshon ke Khilonay*. Alyque gave clear and concise instructions to his actors and I did not have to work too hard on my performance. The play was successful and Alyque set about preparing for another play. This time he chose Arthur Miller's *All My Sons,* which Riffat Shamim had adapted into Urdu as *Sara Sansar Apna Parivar.* I received good reviews for my performance in both plays. I was worried about losing my job with Prithvi Theatre where, as an understudy I received a salary of two hundred and fifty rupees a month, while with the Theatre Group I was not earning a paisa, even though I was their leading lady.

Around the same time I chanced upon a newspaper advertisement for announcers for All India Radio. I asked Sardar Bhai to write out my application and not much later I was called for an interview. Narendra Sharma who was setting up Vividh Bharti, had seen our production of *Sheeshon ke Khiloney*, and had liked my work. I got a job as an announcer with a salary of one hundred and fifty rupees a month. I earned an additional twenty-five rupees for my work in radio plays. Sushma Anand, who later became Vijay Anand's wife, and two young men whose names I cannot recall were selected with me.

It is a matter of some pride for me that Vividh Bharti's first programme of Urdu-Hindi film songs, *Man Chahe Geet* (Much Loved Songs), was broadcast in 1957 with me as the announcer. This was a milestone in the history of Indian broadcasting because after 1947 there had been a ban on film music on the radio, as it was not considered worthy of the national air waves. Instead, film music was heard on the much loved 'Binaca Geet Mala' from Radio Ceylon. In the first few broadcasts we followed a convention of announcing the names of the films and the playback singers. In a meeting with Narendra Sharma and the Station Director, I pointed out that it was unfair not to give due credit to the lyricist and the music director and insisted that we announce their names as well. From that day onwards this became standard practice on Vividh Bharti. When I told Sahir Ludhianvi he was particularly pleased because he was writing most of the top hits of the time.

Around 1961 or 1962 Alyque decided to take his three Urdu plays to Chandigarh. It was around this time that Bare Bhaijan, who was visiting us, invited me to go to Karachi with him. At Partition most of my brothers and sisters had migrated to Pakistan, but Abbajan and Ammajan, my two older sisters and I had decided not to leave India. I was excited at the prospect of meeting my brothers and sisters whom I had not seen in ages. Torn between the Theatre Group's tour and a visit to Pakistan, after some deliberation I decided to visit my family. Riffat Shamim tried to convince Alyque to cast somebody else in my roles but he did not agree; he simply gave up producing Urdu plays.

On my return from Pakistan, Sajjan, a fellow actor from Prithvi Theatre, came to see me and told me that he had started a new theatre group called Triveni Rang Manch. He had written a play called *Pagli* (The Mad Woman) as its inaugural production. It had five male characters and one female who was the central character. Sajjan said to me, 'You are the only actress who can play this role,' and added, 'I want to get the play ready in time for the Maharashtra State Drama Competition.'

'How much time do we have?' I enquired.

'Very little' he said, 'I can give you the script today but we cannot rehearse for more than seven days because all the other actors are doing films and are not very flexible with their dates.' The only name I recall from the cast is that of the well-known film actor, Agha.

The role of the insane woman was very demanding. Kaifi's support and advice proved invaluable: every morning, he would help me memorise my dialogue. I disrupted the entire household while rehearsing. One day I climbed on to a takht and started shouting, 'Stand up, stand up! We are being bombed...take up your weapons!' My cook dropped what he was doing and ran for his life, thinking I had actually gone mad! Shabana, who was ten at the time, began to cry thinking her mother was actually insane. Kaifi took her for a walk to Juhu Beach, and comforted her in the gentle manner that he had reserved specially for her, 'Your mother is not mad, she is preparing for a play. You should feel proud not embarrassed, that she takes her work so seriously. In fact you should help her learn her lines and win the Best Actress Award.' When the play opened it was a hit and I did win the Best Actress award in the All Maharashtra Drama Competition.

I was now working regularly in Sajjan's plays earning fifty rupees per performance. One day, I was getting ready to go on tour and not unusually I was penniless. Kaifi had come to the station to see me off and I asked him for some money but the poor dear was also broke. Frustrated, I shouted, 'I always have to go on tour empty-handed; you never have any money; and my slipper is broken.' Muttering and grumbling I boarded the train. 'Give it to me, I'll have it repaired' said Kaifi, as he secreted my slipper in his wide white kurta sleeve and went off. He returned not much later with the repaired slipper. I was deeply touched and said, 'I'm sorry I was so unpleasant.' Quietly, he handed me fifty rupees. 'O wow, if this doesn't beat everything!' I exclaimed, 'Where did you get this from?'

'Don't ask,' he replied, adding, 'the train is about to leave.' Contrite, I put on my slipper and kissed Kaifi's hand. After the show when I asked Sajjan for my money, surprised, he said, 'But, Kaifi Sahib took it from me at the station.' It was outrageous but my heart went out to the wily Kaifi.

In the years after independence IPTA was covered in dustsheets because the artists were either in jail, or they had moved away, dissatisfied with the misguided policies of the Party, which changed with every new General Secretary. In those days IPTA was run by men like Habib Tanvir and Ahuja for whom the concept of 'people's art' had been reduced to mere sloganeering. In 1950 A.K. Hangal, a member of the Party who had moved to India from Pakistan, took charge of IPTA with R.M. Singh, another Party member. Together they breathed new life into the organization. I did two plays with Hangal Sahib, both of which were well received. In 1957, Hangal Sahib directed a play called *Damru*. The central role was that of a sixty-year old man who worked in a bank, and for this Hangal Sahib took the unusual step of casting Harihar Jariwalla, a young man who was barely twenty-two or twenty-three years old. By now I was a well-established actress and was playing the role of his fifty-year old wife, a woman weighed down by the burden of bringing up her many children. I said to Hangal Sahib, 'You've given a very important role to a very young and inexperienced actor. Will he be able to pull it off?' Hangal Sahib said, 'Shaukatji, you have seen his commitment; he is a dedicated member of the Association, the least we can do is to give him a chance.'

When we started rehearsing I was amazed to see how convincing this young man was as a sixty-year old. When the show opened it was Harihar who caught the audience's imagination. His lines, 'Work hard, brother, work hard! Only then will you get on in life, only then will there be progress, only then will you become human,' were on everybody's lips. His make-up and his demeanour were perfect: no trace of the twenty-three year old betrayed him. After his brilliant performance Harihar was cast in all subsequent IPTA productions where he impressed many writers and directors. Vishwamitra Adil, the General Secretary of IPTA, who was also a screenwriter, decided to introduce Harihar to the film world and took him to meet all the directors that he knew. Though Harihar started his career in B Grade films it was not long before he started working for the big banners. Today the world knows him as Sanjeev Kumar and he is ranked among the best film actors of India. Although he stopped acting in theatre after he moved to films, he kept it touch with his theatre colleagues, and was a regular visitor to our house in Janki Kutir. He was just forty-two years old when he died tragically of a sudden heart attack. I feel his loss to this day.

Vishwamitra Adil was a very dear friend of ours; in fact, he was married to my Choti Apajan's sister-in-law, my old friend Zakia. He had adapted Zul Vellani's *No Other Way* into Urdu. It was an anti-British play set in Africa, called *Afrika Jawan Pareshan* (Africa, Young and Awake). Adil said, 'R.M. Singh is going to direct the play and trust me, this is the role you will be remembered by. Grab it.' I knew at the first reading that Adil was right and set about creating the character, bringing to it all the training I had received at Prithvi.

It is as difficult to put life into a role, as it is to give birth to a baby. I borrowed some books on Africa from Khwaja Ahmad Abbas to research my character. I was drawn to a photograph of a woman with a proud yet tragic face, sitting by a well. I put dark make-up on and as I sat before a mirror, in exactly the same manner as the woman in the photograph, the whole character came to life before my eyes. When I stood up it was not I but she who walked; it was not I who spoke but the African woman in her deep voice. On the first night, members of the audience broke into my Green Room saying, 'We could have sworn that you were from Africa. What an incredible performance!' I got excellent reviews and Anwar Azim of the Urdu Blitz devoted an entire page to my performance. Hangal Sahib played the role of my father-in-law with his usual skill.

Then, as now, the commercial success of a play had more to do with marketing than with its critical worth. We had a very successful tour through India, but were let down by the organizers in Hyderabad. They told us shamefacedly that as only eight people had turned up to watch our play, they thought it best to cancel the performance and reimburse the audience. Both Hangal Sahib and I insisted that the show must go on, and we went on to give one of the finest performances of our careers. Shabana who was witness to this incident told me, 'This was a defining moment in my commitment to theatre. Regardless of all else, every performance is a test the actor must stand up to. The memory of my mother standing before that tiny audience and giving a masterly performance is a talisman that I hold on to.'

After the success of *Afrika Jawan Pareshan*, I was cast in all IPTA productions and did several plays like *Election ka Ticket* (The Election Ticket), translated from English by Adil. *Azar ka Khwab* (Azar's Dream) was an adaptation by Qudsia Zaidi, of Bernard Shaw's *Pygmalion* in which Balraj Sahni played Henry Higgins, and I as Phupi Amma was Mrs. Pearce the housekeeper. In *Lal Gulab Ki Vaapsi* (Return of the Red Rose) written by Khwaja Ahmad Abbas, I played the female lead opposite Balraj Sahni. Sagar Sarhadi had written *Tanhai,* a controversial play based on the life of the actress Leela Chitnis and her difficult relationship with her son. He was keen for me to play the central role. IPTA however was reluctant to go ahead with the production because the character of the leading lady had many negative traits and the protagonists in IPTA's production were always good and heroic. I had no qualms about playing the part and insisted that we go ahead with the play because it was a slice of life. I had to wear sleeveless blouses and flirt outrageously with Hangal Sahib. Baba, who was fourteen, was outraged and he refused to watch the play but Kaifi had no such reservations. I laughed off my son's reaction. In any case, I was hardly going to be swayed by objections and give up my work, which I loved. *Tanhai* was directed by Ramesh Talwar and very well received.

Acting is a very demanding profession because it requires the actor to immerse herself in her part and yet maintain a watchful distance. In the play *Aakhri Sawal* (The Final Question) I was cast in the heartbreaking role of Dr Mukta who has to watch her young daughter die of cancer. Prithvirajji had taught us to merge ourselves completely with the parts we were playing. Perhaps I took his advice too seriously. Playing Dr Mukta took a toll on my health because for me the boundary between art and life became blurred. I became obsessed with the thought of my daughter Shabana suffering from this dreadful disease. Kaifi who watched me going to pieces was alarmed and said to Ramesh Talwar, 'Please, have mercy on me and spare my wife.' Ramesh Talwar closed down the play.

I had all but given up theatre when in 1983 Kaifi, who was the All India President of IPTA, invited the very talented Ranjit Kapur to come from Delhi to Bombay and direct a play for IPTA. Ranjit chose *Enter a Freeman* and persuaded me to return to acting, after a considerable gap. He cast Satish Kaushik, who was young enough to be my son, as my husband and to his credit Satish did more than justice to the part. Today, Satish is a very successful film director. I was very impressed by Ranjit and would happily have done more work with him, but my health was failing. I could not give the commitment that acting, and particularly theatre, requires. *Enter a Freeman* was my last play. Over the years I have had to turn down several offers for theatre and film roles, and I do this with some regret. Naseeruddin

Shah, who is India's leading theatre and film actor, has tried to cajole me back to theatre. While it is very heartening for me to have my favourite actor asking me to perform in his productions, I cannot find the energy to go back to work.

8

The Silver Screen

A round 1970 M.S. Sathyu, Abu Shivani and Ishan Arya, all friends from IPTA, formed a company called 3MM and decided to make a film. They selected one of Ismat Apa's short stories and sent it to the Film Finance Corporation who turned it down. Kaifi was asked to step in, adapt the story and write a screenplay: a task that he completed in less than a week. The Film Finance Corporation was approached again and this time they agreed to finance the production. Sathyu was selected as the Director, Ishan Arya the cameraman and Abu Shivani the Producer. Kaifi and I went to Balraj Sahni to offer him the main role, but when he heard the story he was apprehensive, 'Do you think I'll be able to pull off this Muslim character?' I said, 'You've played roles as diverse as a helpless farmer in *Do Bigha Zamin* and a Pathan in *Kabuli Wala* most convincingly; this role is far less demanding.' After much persuasion he agreed. To prepare for the part Balrajji spent many days with a Muslim comrade and his family in Bhiwandi. He observed the comrade's father closely, paying special attention to how he performed his ablutions and offered his prayers. Balrajji had started living the part before facing the camera.

The shooting commenced in an old haveli in Agra. As most of the actors were from IPTA, there was a healthy camaraderie on the sets. Despite the fact that he was a big star Balraj Sahni hung around the sets even when he was not shooting and put everyone at ease.

We were like a large family and there was an absence of the hierarchy that is usual on film sets.

Sathyu's emphasis was on realism, devoid of all melodrama. Kaifi's scenes were so true to life that the actors could speak their lines effortlessly. Kaifi drew upon his own relationship with Shabana for the scenes between Balrajji and his daughter, played by Gita Hattangadi. The conversations between Farooque Shaikh and Gita who played brother and sister in the film, could well have been between Baba and Shabana. I had little trouble playing my character because I modelled it largely on my mother. But the scene where I rip apart my dead daughter's shroud wrenched my insides.

An incident from Ammajan's life had moved me profoundly. After he retired, Abbajan returned to his ancestral home in Lohari, where they had a three-storeyed house to which Ammajan had a special attachment, because it was here that she had first stepped out of her bridal palanquin. Now, Abbajan's sister lived in this house with her family and he had made it quite clear that he was not going to ask her to move out. Much against her wishes Ammajan had to live nearby in a house built of mud. In her last days she said to Abbajan, 'I will not die in peace unless I return to my own house; please, take me to my room just once.' It was after Bare Bhaijan carried Ammajan in his arms to the room where she had come as a young bride that she was able to breathe her last. Kaifi put this episode into the script of *Garm Hawa* almost exactly as I had related it to him.

Garm Hawa was made on a shoestring budget and under many technical constraints. Ishan Arya had to make do with only five lights, but he was an exceptional cinematographer, and turned this handicap into an asset. He did away with reflectors for outdoor shoots, and instead used a white sheet, which was less harsh on the actors' eyes. He was one of the first people to use this technique in India, although today it is the norm. We could not afford the professional 'nagra' to record the dialogue and had to make do with an ordinary cassette recorder. When it came to doing the post-synch sound, we did not have a proper soundtrack for reference. All the actors had to synchronize their dialogue to the lip movement on screen, without the help of a pilot or guide track. Balrajji was so impressed by Sathyu's work that during the dubbing he would often say, 'After the release of this film even Satyajit Ray will have to sport a beard' because Sathyu has one.' Alas, Balrajji who had not taken a single day off during the shoot and had worked with a passion for four months did not see the completed film because he died of a heart attack one day after he had finished dubbing for the film. He was correct; *Garm Hawa* is a highly acclaimed film that has won many awards, including a National Award for Kaifi. It remains the definitive film on the effects of Partition on the lives of Muslims of north India.

When Muzaffar Ali started work on *Umrao Jaan* (1981) he offered me Khanam's role. I was more interested in playing Umrao's mother, but Subhashini who was Muzaffar's wife at the time, impressed upon me that Umrao's mother is a lacklustre and helpless woman whereas Khanam who is a strong, autonomous and impressive woman is a far more interesting character to portray. I am glad I took Subhashini's advice because to this day I get praise for my performance as Khanam, a worldly woman who runs the premiere salon of courtesans in Lucknow. In fact, after watching the film Kaifi told Subhashini, 'Shaukat is so convincing as Khanam that had I seen the film before I married her I would have investigated her family tree!'

After *Umrao Jaan* I worked in several other films such as *Bazaar* (dir. Sagar Sarhadi, 1982), which explores the tragedy of young Indian girls who are 'sold' into marriage to rich Arabs from the Gulf. *Lorie* (dir. Vijay Talwar, 1984) is a compelling story about a young woman, Geeta Malhotra (played by Shabana), who loses her first child and is unable to have another. I played the mother of the child Geeta kidnaps and brings up as her own. I worked with Muzaffar Ali for the second time in *Anjuman* (1986). Even though I play the role of a trouble-making busybody, this film is close to my heart because it is the story of SEWA, a self-help organization for women that trains them in chikan embroidery and markets the finished goods for them. Shabana plays Anjuman, the young woman who galvanizes the chikan embroidery workers in Lucknow, in a struggle to transform their lives.

One morning, in 1988, Mira Nair arrived at my house in Janki Kutir and said, 'Shaukat Apa, I am making a film called, *Salaam Bombay*. I would like you to act in it.' By now I had given up acting because of chronic health problems and showed little interest, though I did ask her what the film was about. She narrated the story in some detail and told me that the film was about the prostitutes of Kamati Pura, and offered me the role of the Madam of the brothel. Trying to slip out of doing the role, I said, 'Madam of the brothel! I have never set eyes on such a creature.' Shabana called out from inside, 'Mummy, you must do her film; she is a good Director.' I asked Mira about her earlier work and she told me at some length about a documentary that she had made on cabaret dancers. 'I shall give you a videocassette that you must watch. You will see how I went into their homes and filmed them, even though I had to face many difficulties including police harassment—but we got away with making the film.'

Now, I was interested and asked Mira, 'What makes you think that I can play this role?'

'I have seen you in *Garm Hawa*.'

I looked at her perplexed, '*Garm Hawa*! The two characters could not be more different!'

She laughed and said, 'You give yourself completely to your part. It's not as though you're trying to prove, "Look this is I, Shaukat Kaifi, playing this role!"'

My interest was further aroused, 'I am not sure I can play this role because I have no idea what that world is like.'

She persisted, 'I shall take you there and introduce you to these women who are wonderful. I have been working with them for the past year and a half, and am also running a workshop for twenty-five children.'

The following afternoon I went with Mira to Kamati Pura, Bombay's famous red light district. My eyes were searching for a role model whom I found sitting under a tree. I observed her very carefully. She was a middle-aged woman who was busy playing cards with a male friend. I went up to speak to her, and saw that her arm was burnt and she was trying to hide an ugly scar. I could not bear the sleaziness that permeated the atmosphere and left hastily. This was certainly not a project for the fainthearted. I decided to face the challenge. The following week I re-visited Kamati Pura several times with Mira.

When we started shooting Mira booked two rooms in a nearby hotel for make-up and other facilities. On the first day, when I descended the stairs all made up, nobody could recognize me. Mira was pleased with my first shot, as was Sandi Sissell, the camerawoman who was from the United States. I knew I had succeeded in portraying the character when the local prostitutes laughed and said, 'Lordy, can it be true that she's Shabana Azmi's mother? She's a real Madam! Look at that brazen expression in her eyes!' After the shoot Kaifi came to pick me up and I got into the car without bothering to remove my make-up or change my clothes. He looked at me and said very quietly, 'You could at least have spared a thought for my reputation.'

All the art film producers and directors knew that I was a senior stage actress and accorded me due respect. However, working on commercial films was a different matter altogether. I had a small role in a film called *Prince* (dir. Lekh Tandon, 1969) starring Shammi Kapoor, who was Prithvirajji's son and a matinee idol, famous for his unique style of dancing, which was a blend of rock-n-roll, the twist and Indian dance styles. When I arrived at the studio I was informed that I had to use the junior artistes' make-up room, shared by both men and women. I put on my make-up and went on the set without making a fuss. When my first shot was 'okayed' in the first take, everyone sat up and took notice. At lunch, Tandon's assistant Randhir Kapoor, who is Papaji's grandson and the legendary actor/

director Raj Kapoor's eldest son, learnt that I was sharing a dressing room with junior artistes. He was furious and arranged for me to have a separate dressing room. I was pleased because I have always believed that my work will speak for itself.

9

Janki Kutir

In 1959 we were forced to leave Red Flag Hall because it belonged to Harkishan Das Hospital and the management wanted it back. Once again it fell upon Kaifi to find a place for us to live. Kaifi had a very wide circle of acquaintance that included people from across the social divide. It was through a son-in-law of the wealthy Birlas that he found a cottage in Janki Kutir in Juhu for two hundred and twenty rupees a month. It belonged to Jamnalal Bajaj, another wealthy industrialist. Although we were sad to leave Red Flag Hall, we were excited to move to Janki Kutir because Mahatama Gandhi had often lived in the area. On 15th September, two days after we celebrated Baba's sixth birthday, we moved to our new house where three days later on 18th September we celebrated Shabana's ninth birthday.

After twelve years of married life this was the first time that I was going to live in a 'real' house with two rooms and a separate kitchen, and I was elated. Both Kaifi and I wanted an attractive and convivial home but how to achieve this was a source of constant bickering between us. I would say one thing and he another. I thought his suggestions were harebrained while he thought mine outlandish. Finally we reached a compromise: Kaifi would take charge of the garden and I would look after the interior. Most importantly, it was agreed that we would not interfere in each other's territories. The house had no privacy nor did it have any space where we could entertain guests. I decided to convert the verandah into a living room and had a three-foot high wall built, but ran out of money to have it plastered and had to leave the bricks bare. Kaifi and I went beach-combing to Juhu where we picked some pebbles and small shells. I stuck these between the bricks, and created a wall which was so charming, that to this day I have not had it plastered. I had a trellis fixed above the wall. Even today, after nearly half a century this verandah remains our living room.

We now had to deal with the problems of schools for the children. Shabana was unwilling to bid goodbye to Queen Mary's. For the first three months Alice accompanied her to school every morning. Soon Shabana became so independent that she travelled to school and back on her own. Her school was fourteen kilometers away from Juhu, and nine-year old Shabana went by bus to Santa Cruz station, from where she took a local train to Grant Road station and then walked for fifteen minutes to reach school. My sister Qamar who was living in Nigeria at the time, wrote me a letter, admonishing me in no uncertain terms, 'You are a very cruel mother for sending such a little girl to school on her own.' She did not know that every evening, at six o'clock when it was time for Shabana to return home I would sit on the front lawn and wait for her. If for some reason she was late I would feel faint and make a thousand pledges, begging God to bring my Shabana home safe. Baba's school, Hill Grange, was at Pedder Road, which was very far from Janki Kutir. The school bus did not come to Juhu and we had to find a new school nearer home for six-year old Baba. It was difficult for me to travel the long distance to the Radio Station, and so I resigned from my job.

ॐ

Janki Kutir has always been an open house, where all festivals such as Eid, Diwali, Holi and Christmas are celebrated with equal joy. It became a hangout for members of IPTA, Kaifi's workers from

Madanpura, famous and not-so-famous poets, stragglers from Shabana's Film Institute and Baba's friends.

Janki Kutir had basic creature comforts and no 'attached bathrooms'. Nevertheless, our steady stream of guests included poets of the stature of Firaq Gorakhpuri, Josh Malihabadi and Faiz Ahmed Faiz. I always did my best to make our guests comfortable and it was not unusual for me to pawn my solitary gold bangle, for some extra cash. When I had the money I would retrieve the bangle, and wear it till the next emergency. Josh Sahib enjoyed chicken qorma with parathas for breakfast. All we could afford was a kerosene stove and it took ages for anything to cook on it. One morning, as I was preparing Josh Sahib's breakfast, the chicken was taking ages to cook. Josh Sahib was most gracious and instead of getting prickly because he had to wait interminably for his breakfast, he would ask Kaifi most solicitously, 'Do you think I should have another gilauri?' His paans were wrapped up in a red cloth and kept with some jasmine flowers in a silver box, and as he would mention the word his attendant would present him with one. Finally the qorma was ready and I tied a bib round Josh Sahib's neck to protect his clothes. I remember how nervous I was to have kept him waiting, but he put me at ease by declaring, 'Kaifi, your wife has produced an excellent qorma!'

On one of his visits Kaifi had organized a baithak for Josh Sahib. As he was reciting his verse there were cries of 'vah! vah!' but the gentleman sitting opposite him had a vacant expression because he was unfamiliar with the finer points of the Urdu language. Josh Sahib summoned Kaifi and whispered in his ear, 'Please, move that man, each misra of mine hits his forehead and boomerangs back at me!' Poor Kaifi had to summon all his tact to move the offending guest.

It was Kaifi's way to come to me scratching his head, as he informed me that he had invited some people for dinner. I would ask, 'How many?' and he would mumble, 'About ten to fifteen.'

'Goodness, Kaifi, it's four o' clock! Why didn't you tell me in the morning?' I would protest, 'at least I'd have had some time to make proper arrangements.'

He would say, 'I was scared that you'd be furious.' Holding my head in despair I would get down to work. It was a miracle that we never ran short.

ভচ

It was 1960 and I was working with Alyque Padamsee when Bare Bhaijan who was a senior official in the Customs and Excise Department in Karachi decided to visit Bombay. He invited me to go back to Pakistan with him. In Karachi I basked in the generous love showered upon me by my brothers and sisters, who did everything they possibly could to make my visit a memorable one. My cousin Akbar, who a decade and a half earlier had smuggled Kaifi's letters to me, took me to see the now ruined ancient city of Thatta with his wife Akhtar. I was amazed to see how women had embroidered exquisite floral and geometric motifs – without any patterns or drawings – on coloured fabric. I fell in love with the stunning textiles. My younger brother, Nasrullah Khan who was a bank manager in Hyderabad Sindh took time off from work to take me around the city. With endless patience he took me to the old bazaars, where I bought many typical Sindhi mirror work embroideries. Actually, I did not have the money to buy anything, all my shopping was done courtesy my brothers and sisters. I must confess to a weakness for Pakistani salimshahi shoes, particularly those from Peshawar and Multan, with exquisite gold and silver zari embroidery that does not tarnish, even after years of wear and tear. Nawabjani bought me a dozen pairs which I accepted without the slightest protest.

I spent three months in Pakistan and returned to Bombay with my younger sister Qamar, who was betrothed to Dr Shehryar and wanted to buy her trousseau in India. From the deck of the ship I spotted my poor husband with a child on either side, waiting for me at the quayside. I disembarked, bedecked with gold jewellery and bearing three suitcases full of gifts. Seven year old Baba exclaimed, 'How can this woman laden with gold be my Mummy!' I had been away from the family for an awfully long time and the house was in complete disarray. Kaifi, who had to go to Calcutta in connection with some film, barely had any clothes. My brothers had given me a thousand rupees, which I spent on four sets of kurta pyjamas for him. The Sindhi textiles soon came in handy. I used them for the costumes I designed for Heer for the film *Heer Ranjha*, even though it was difficult for me to part with them.

In several subsequent visits to Pakistan with Kaifi I had the opportunity to meet the dynamic literary community of the country. It delighted me that Kaifi was toasted in Pakistan in much the same manner that Faiz was in India. People's love of Urdu poetry transcended political and geographical boundaries. I have always returned from Pakistan marvelling at how little difference there is between the people of my own country India, and the people there, except perhaps, that Pakistanis are more hospitable.

10

Shabana and Baba

My children have always been both my strength and my weakness. While I have encouraged them to speak their minds without fear, I set great store by courtesy and appearances. Even though our budget was always over-stretched the children were extremely well turned out. One day, rummaging through Kaifi's papers I found an old letter of mine, written when on tour with Prithvi Theatre. It is addressed to the two-year-old Shabana but is actually directed at Kaifi with whom I was cross about something.

22 January 1952
Vijayawada

My dearest Nono Betey,
I was cleaning my attaché case when out fell a photograph of yours, which your Abba had sent to me when I was in Kashmir. My, was I thrilled! I say, your ribbon looks very grand, particularly with that lock of hair covering one of your adorable eyes. And my goodness, that watch on your wrist looks very expensive; I must say that even I cannot afford to buy one. And who put your sweater on for you? The little flowers on it look very fetching, as does your face. I want to kiss you; I miss you so much that I want to cry. And Nono has the water dried in your river? And how did the monkey bite in Rani Bagh? Like this? Upon my soul, I am petrified. What does the old man say? He says, 'Allah, please give

me this child. Tell the old man, 'No, no, no; go away. Our child is very special to us. We are not parting with her.' And Betey, what was it that you said to me, 'Mummy, don't go to work because then Abba has to make tea. Betey, this Boss of mine is dreadful; he forces me to work. I shall come back soon and kiss my Lappu Mappu. Now, first tell me, whose beta are you? Mummy's! Oho! My precious beta, who's Kuchu Muchu are you? Mummy's! Oho! My Kuchu Muchu, now tell me Nono, how are you? Is your rash still itching? Do you take your medicine regularly? How is your Abba? Does he look after you properly or is he roaming around wasting time? Do you get proper food or not? Write in detail.

I have bought a small pastry board and rolling pin for you, so now you will not have to borrow Yusuf's and can make your own rotis. And yes, tell your Abba that on 27th or 28th January, your Aunty Amina is coming especially to see you and give you a big hug. Abba should buy you a pair of shoes from Bata and white socks too. Tell your ayah that she should dress you up in your light blue frilly skirt and the white organza blouse, which should be perfectly ironed. Tie white ribbons in your hair on both sides. Betey you must greet your Aunty with a proper salaam and be very hospitable. Ask Abba to get whatever you need. The house must be spotlessly clean. There are two light green curtains: use one as a bed cover and the other as a tablecloth for the writing table. Have the brass flower vase scrubbed with ash and polished till it sparkles. Make sure the plants are watered every fifteen days or else my precious plants will wilt and die. Well Betey, now I must say goodbye because I have to get back to work. I hold you tight, close to my heart and shower you with a billion kisses.

    Ta ta
    From
    Your Loving Mummy

P.S. Give your Abba my salam provided he is not making arrangements for another mother for you.

There were rather a lot of instructions for a two year old! Hopefully, Kaifi took note of the postscript.

∞

Alice the ayah was a godsend and she was always thinking of new ways to keep the children entertained. Every evening she would kit out Shabana and Baba and take them to the Chowpatty. A few years ago Shabana told me that when she was six and Baba three, Alice used to take them to a Parsi wedding hall near our house and let them have their fill of free ice cream and cold drinks. It was not long before the watchman became suspicious and demanded 'How come you are related to every family that is having a wedding? Now, get lost and don't come here again—buzz off or I shall report the matter to the big boss.' Nonplussed, Alice led the children away mumbling, 'Arrey, what the hell do you lose if the children get something to eat. Really, what cheek! Getting angry like this; he stuffs himself and that's all right!' And sadly, the children's month of free treats came to an end.

သည်

As a little girl Shabana was convinced that I loved Baba more than I loved her. Perhaps, there was some truth in this because Baba's arrival had filled some of the void left by Khayyam's death. One morning, when Shabana was nine years old and Baba just six, I was giving them their breakfast and picked up a toast from Shabana's plate, saying, 'Betey, Baba's bus will be here soon, so I am giving this toast to him. You have a little more time; I've sent Alice to get some bread and she'll be back any minute.' Shabana left the table silently. When Alice returned I called out, 'Shabana, Shabana, come Betey, look your toast is done.' I heard her in the bathroom, sobbing as though her heart would break, and rushed to her. The moment she saw me, Shabana hastily wiped away her tears and left for school. She went to the laboratory and took some nila thotha. Mercifully, the poison had passed its sell-by date. I held my head in despair when Parna, Shabana's best friend from their kindergarten days told me that Shabana had told her, 'Mummy loves Baba more than she loves me.'

I recall another incident when I told Shabana off quite firmly, because she had been rude to me, only to discover that she had tried to throw herself in front of a train at Grant Road station. Luckily, her school's janitor happened to be standing behind her and managed to pull her back, shouting, 'Baby, Baby what are you doing?' Shabana escaped a second time but I was most distraught and now had to think twice before telling her off. It was her hypersensitivity that also made her acutely aware of our financial constraints, and she never made the usual demands that most children make of their parents. White plimsoles were a part of her uniform and Shabana went through a pair in three or four months. One day, I grumbled, 'Such large feet like clodhoppers! How can I afford a new pair, every three months?' A few days later I noticed that her shoe was ripped near the small toe, but instead of asking for a new pair Shabana had cut out a piece of cardboard and glued it on the hole. My heart went out to her and I scraped together some money and bought her a new pair. I used to give Shabana thirty paisa a day for her bus fare from Juhu to Santa Cruz station. If she wanted a snack she saved five paisas by getting off the bus four stops earlier at Juhu Chowpatty and trudging home, but she never demanded extra money. Once again, it was from Parna that I learnt about this many years later.

Shabana was always looking for ways to earn some extra money for the house. After she had passed her Senior Cambridge in the first division, Shabana had three months before going to college. She found herself a job selling Bru Coffee at petrol stations, earning thirty rupees a day. She did not tell me, and I am afraid that I was so busy rehearsing that I did not notice her absence. At the end of the month she handed me all the money she had earned. Surprised, I asked, 'Betey, where did you get this money from?' She made light of it and said, 'I had three months to wait before going to college. I thought, why not put the time to some use.' I was very proud of Shabana but I was also distraught that at this young age she felt she had to share her family's financial responsibilities.

It is not entirely surprising that Shabana has grown into the responsible and caring activist that she is today. From her childhood she was present at gatherings where progressive intellectuals discussed and debated current affairs and the human condition. She

enjoyed hanging around poets and writers like Sajjad Zaheer, Josh
Malihabadi, Faiz Ahmad Faiz and Firaq Gorakhpuri who were our
regular houseguests. Kaifi often arranged mehfils for them and other
visiting artists like Begum Akhtar. Often Shabana would accompany
Kaifi to his trade union meetings where she loved being pampered
by the labourers.

∞

Although Shabana continued to be a good student at St. Xavier's
College her heart was in acting. She formed the Hindi Theatre Group
with Farooque Shaikh who was two years her senior, and together
they won all the awards in the Inter-Collegiate Drama Competitions.
After graduating Shabana asked Kaifi if he would object to her
taking up acting as a career and Kaifi said, 'I'll support any choice
you make. If you choose to become a cobbler I shall support you,
provided you become the best cobbler in the business.' Shabana
enrolled in the acting course at the Film and Television Institute in
Pune in 1971 and won the Atmaram Scholarship of two hundred
and fifty rupees for best student, which looked after her fees. She
completed her diploma with a distinction and was awarded a gold
medal for best student in acting in the class of 1973.

I loved Shabana's work in her first film, Shyam Benegal's *Ankur*
(The Seeding, 1974) and I was delighted to hear her get the Hyderabadi
dialect just right. She looked every inch a village girl even though she
had never been near a village before the filming started. I was not
surprised when she won the National Award for best actress for this
performance. Next I saw her in K.A. Abbas's *Faslah* (1974) opposite
Raman Kumar who was also the producer of the film. Never one for
mincing my words, I told her, 'You were a disaster; plus your clothes
and your hairstyle were horrid. Thank your stars I saw you in *Ankur*
before this or else I would have married you off to the first available
man, and spared the film industry the burden of putting up with
you.' Shabana took my comments on the chin because she knew that
the film was a dud.

At the Film Institute Shabana had been exposed to the best of international and Indian cinema. Her natural inclination was always towards art films but she took a decision to work in mainstream cinema as well because as she said, 'Art cinema has a small audience and I hope acting in commercial films will make me "star enough" for audiences to be won over into watching my art films.' It is to her credit that she managed to do both successfully, although I have always preferred Shabana in her art films. I am very proud of her body of work as an actress. Amongst her many accolades she has won five National Awards, of which three were in a row: a feat unparalleled by any actor to this day. Shabana wears her laurels lightly. I can see that she has absorbed many of my habits, paying the same attention to detail that I did. Weeks before she starts shooting for a new film, much like me she is seen walking around the house in the clothes of the character she is playing; one day she is a slum dweller another day a witch, a third day the Godmother. Shabana makes her own choices but if she is confused whether to take on a film or not she will invariably go by the advice I give her, not as a mother to a daughter but as one actress to another.

ॐ

In 1985 Shabana went to Calcutta for the shooting of Gautam Ghose's film *Paar,* which is about a poor couple from a village in Bihar, who come to the city in search of work. She was staying at a guesthouse and decided to observe Rama, the young sweeper woman, in order to prepare for her role. In the process they became friends and Rama invited her home. Shabana told me, 'I had never come across such poverty. Rama lived with eight people in a small room with no electricity and no air. I was astonished to see how someone who lived on so little was capable of such generosity. I felt that if I went back to Bombay and forgot all about her it would be a travesty of the trust she had placed in me as a friend. I can't "use" her to win a National Award and then forget all about her.' I looked at Shabana in wonder, because I could hear Kaifi speaking through his daughter.

Coincidentally, soon after she had finished shooting *Paar* Shabana saw Anand Patwardhan's documentary *Bombay Our City*, which is about slum dwellers. The film highlights the fact that people migrate to the city in search of employment, and therefore demolishing their homes would serve no purpose, because they would not return to their villages but simply move a few kilometers away to another slum. Shabana joined an organization called Nivara Hakk (Right to Shelter), which works for the slum dwellers of Bombay.

In May 1986 a twenty-five year old slum in Colaba, called Sanjay Gandhi Nagar was razed to the ground, heartlessly. In protest, four slum dwellers and Anand Patwardhan decided to go on hunger strike. Shabana felt she could not abandon them at this critical time and decided to join them, even though the following day she was supposed to go to the Cannes Film Festival for Mrinal Sen's film *Genesis*. Her husband Javed cautioned her, saying 'You are a famous actress, people will attribute all kinds of motives to you, and may accuse you of being a publicity hound. If you can face that, go ahead because the slum dwellers will benefit greatly by your joining their struggle.' I went weak in the knees and was not in favour of an indefinite hunger strike, but I had to keep my peace. Kaifi was in Patna and when Shabana telephoned her Abba to inform him of her decision, he said, 'Best of luck, Comrade.'

In the early hours of the appointed morning Shabana embraced everyone at home and joined the strike. I went to visit the hunger strikers and my blood ran cold. Five people were lying in a constricted space, by the roadside, on a makeshift wooden platform with no mattress and no pillows, and among them was my Shabana. Some tattered sheets had been tied to bamboo poles and held up as an apology for a canopy, which was scant protection from the scorching sun. I did not want my child to lose heart, so I controlled my tears, put on a brave smile and joined the sloganeers, shouting, 'Stop showing your might, a home is our right!' By the fourth day of the strike my spirit broke and I stood by helplessly praying, 'Please God, let these people succeed in their mission.' I returned home in tears.

On the fifth day, the actor Shashi Kapoor, a close family friend, and Papaji's youngest son, came to visit Shabana, who by now had become very weak with a sharp drop in her blood pressure. Shashi went to see the Chief Minister S.B. Chavan and pleaded, 'When you have needed the film fraternity to raise funds and have asked us to do charity shows, we have never refused. But now when one of us is struggling between life and death you remain unmoved.' The Chief Minister responded by ordering that the hunger strikers' demands be met. The housing minister who had been deaf to their demands now decreed that the hunger strikers be given orange juice. The strike was called off; and I was thankful that my child's life was saved. Land was found as compensation for the residents of Sanjay Gandhi Nagar.

This was Shabana's first step as a social activist. Since then she has worked tirelessly for housing rights, basic amenities, schools and health facilities for more than fifty slum colonies in Mumbai. In 2007 Nivara Hakk, of which Shabana is President, built 12,000 homes at no cost for the slum dwellers ousted from the National Park. Shabana's collegues, architect P.K. Das, who designed the project, journalist Gurbir Singh and social worker Anna Kurien, braved lathi charges and courted arrest countless times. It was after an eight-year struggle that the task was accomplished. Shabana tells me that there was a three-way agreement arrived at between the Government of Maharashtra, a private builder, Sumer Corporation and Nivara Hakk. This is the largest single rehabilitation project in Asia. Kaifi had written the poem 'Makaan', a lament for the homeless, forty-five years ago. It is in the fitness of things that his daughter's work resonates with the sentiments Kaifi expressed so deeply.

The second turning point in Shabana's political life was the brutal murder of Safdar Hashmi, a social activist who was the director of a well-known street theatre group, Jan Natya Manch. He was killed in broad daylight by political gangsters during the performance of a revolutionary street play on 1st January, 1989. Not much later there was an International Film Festival in Delhi where Shabana's first English film, *Madame Sousatzka* was opening the festival and John Schlesinger, the director, was present. When Shabana went up on stage and took the microphone in her hand, people thought she was going to say something about her film, but very courageously she said, 'On the one hand the government holds international film festivals and on the other, when a brilliant cultural activist, Safdar Hashmi is brutally murdered by political goons of the party in power, the government takes no action.' H.K.L. Bhagat, the Minister for Information and Broadcasting, who was sitting in the audience rushed on to the stage, furiously grabbed the microphone from Shabana's hand, and declared that everything she had said was untrue, and a lot else. We were watching the proceedings on television in Bombay. Javed and Kaifi were impressed by Shabana's courage but I was worried. Most of the print media applauded Shabana's courage, but H.K.L Bhagat was able to stop her appearance on all radio and television channels, as they were owned by the state. Shabana's face disappeared from the TV screen. It took the intervention of the Prime Minister, Rajiv Gandhi for the restriction to be lifted.

Shabana was trying hard to balance her activism with her profession but in my mind there was no confusion that she was first an actress and then an activist. Hours before she was scheduled to perform her play *Tumhari Amrita* with Farooque Shaikh at the National Centre for the Performing Arts in Bombay, Shabana was arrested along with sixteen slum dwellers on charges of rioting during a demolition which Nivara Hakk activists were trying to prevent. Shabana refused to accept bail arguing that the charges were trumped up. Meanwhile, at the theatre, members of the audience were in their seats, waiting for the curtain to go up. I went up on stage and said, 'Shabana has been arrested and unfortunately, the performance will be delayed. We are sorry for the inconvenience. Those of you who would like to leave, the organizers will reimburse you for your tickets.' Not one member of the audience accepted the offer, and I rushed off with Kaifi to the police station. I pleaded with Shabana, 'Betey, you have an audience waiting for you; the show must go on! You must accept bail if only for a few hours. You can do the play and then return to the police station if you wish.' Shabana was swayed. She reached the theatre and gave an electrifying performance. The actors received a standing ovation from an audience that had waited patiently for over two hours for the show to begin.

Shabana continued with her acting and political activism with complete commitment and ten years later in August 1997 on the recommendation of Prime Minister Sri I.K. Gujral she was nominated by the President Sri Venkatraman, to the Rajya Sabha, the Upper House as a Member of Parliament. In her six year tenure as an MP, Shabana proved to be every bit her father's daughter; raising issues on housing, public health, women's empowerment and education. She was particularly vocal against religious fundamentalism of all kinds.

Members of Parliament have an annual allocation of rupees two crores at their disposal, for spending on development projects. When Shabana became an MP, the rule stated that the funds could only be used in the MP's home province. Shabana argued that members of Parliament nominated by the President should be permitted to use their funds for the uplift of any part of the country. She succeeded in having the rule changed and was able to spend her funds for projects in Bombay, Azamgarh, Jaunpur and Lucknow. In Bombay the Bandra waterfront near Carter Road and Bandstand was a waste dump and Shabana used her MP funds to transform this into a beautiful four-mile long promenade. Juhu Beach was filthy and I brought this to Shabana's attention, 'Betey when I go for my morning walk I see such squalor on Juhu Beach. In Bombay there are many recreational facilities for the rich, such as five star hotels and clubs, but there are hardly any places for the poor, who actually need open spaces far more than the rich, because they live such congested lives.' Now, Juhu Beach is beautiful and clean and for this I must thank my daughter, the architect P.K. Das, the actor Hema Malini, who contributed from her MP funds, and the Juhu Citizens' Welfare Committee.

త౦

In Mijwan a much needed road and bridge that Shabana had constructed across the Kunwar River is a lifeline for more than twenty-five villages, which would get cut off from the highway every year during the monsoon. The well-known Shibli College, in Azamgarh is a co-educational institution, and though it has a large number of female students their hostel facilities were hopelessly inadequate. Shabana used her MP funds to build a new wing in the girls' hostel, which was later named The Kaifi Azmi Girls' Hostel. In recognition of her services to the city, the U.P. government has named a road after her in Azamgarh.

∞

Shabana has boundless energy and it never ceases to surprise me, how despite her many commitments, she finds time to be such a wonderfully attentive daughter. In 1997 I was in Calcutta with Kaifi for a mushaira. Shabana and Javed who were there as well, came to visit me in my hotel room. They saw that I was lying in bed with my face covered. When Kaifi told them that I was suffering some discomfort in my chest, both husband and wife rushed to the reception and called for a doctor who advised them that I should be admitted to hospital immediately. Shabana contacted my heart specialist, Dr B.K. Goyal, who advised her that if I was fit enough to travel I should be flown to Bombay. Shabana and Jadu brought me to Bombay where I was admitted into hospital. There was a narrowing in five of my arteries, and one was virtually blocked. The doctor gave me the option of an angioplasty or bypass surgery, and I decided that I would undergo surgery the very next day. Shabana and Jadu had to arrange for everything overnight. Dr Bhattacharya, one of the best heart surgeons in the country, assured them that the risk involved was as much as that of a pedestrian's chances of meeting with a road accident. Arrangements had to be made for six bottles of blood. Baba and Javed's son Farhan were among the many young people who donated blood. As they were wheeling me into the operation theatre Shabana started singing Faiz's poem, *If, I believed...* to me. I interrupted her and asked her to sing Govinda's song, *I saw your dad at Bandra station*. Shabana did and I joined in robustly, while the doctors wondered how either of us could be related to Kaifi Azmi!

By God's grace the operation was successful. When I regained consciousness I found myself in an intensive care unit with Shabana standing near me wiping away her tears. A young doctor said to me, 'You were so brave during your surgery why is Shabana crying so much?' I said, 'She is my daughter and loves me a great deal.' I was in the ICU for five days and every night Shabana would steal in and sleep on the bare floor. She had no thought for her home or her work and was determined that she would not leave the hospital until I had been nursed back to health. Shabana's friend Bharti Gandhi sent such deliciously light meals for me that I was spared the horrors of hospital food, and for this I remain eternally grateful to her. After twenty-one days, the doctor gave me a clean bill of health and Shabana who had not left my side for a single day, took me back to her place. I find it remarkable that not once during our time in hospital did her husband Javed complain that he was being neglected or that their home was in shambles.

I often marvel at the little boy whom I first saw at the Progressive Writers' Conference in 1949, as he was climbing over the backs of chairs, and count myself fortunate that Jadu, who is warm, witty and compassionate, is my son-in-law. His poem *'Bhook'* (Hunger) has the power to move me to tears. Kaifi considered him the best amongst contemporary Urdu poets. I know that there could be no better partner for Shabana. Over the years my relationship with Shabana has evolved in a way that is difficult to describe. Perhaps, it would be correct to say that now our roles are reversed. Once I used to carry her on my back, take her to work and look after her, now she is watchful of all my needs. I feel that Shabana has become my mother.

᳉

My son Baba has always loved animals and kept pets ranging from dogs, cats, turtles, pigeons, love birds and some I cannot even remember. Once, when he was about seven, a wounded butterfly flew into his room, fell on the floor and died. Baba came to me sobbing as though his heart would break, 'Mummy, if you don't bring the butterfly back to life I will not go to school.' I was taken aback but in a sudden flash of inspiration I said, 'Betey, I shall put the butterfly on a flower and its essence will flow through the butterfly's legs into its body and give it strength. And then, it will fly away.' The poor lamb went off to school with complete faith in my words.

I treasure the fact that my son is so sensitive, but sometimes Baba stretches his compassion to such limits that I get exasperated. In 1960 when I was leaving for my first trip to Pakistan, Kaifi had come with the children to see me off at the harbour. The ship was about to leave when Baba noticed a bit of a sari sticking out of my suitcase. His heart went out to the sari, 'Mummy, open the suitcase immediately, the sari is choking to death.' I tried to reason with him, 'A sari is not a living creature, besides my ship is about to leave, I shall fix it later,' but there was no appeasing Baba. Finally, I had to give in, open my suitcase and pack the sari properly. Just as well that I did not miss my boat in the process of saving the sari's life!

Before going to Pakistan I had given Shabana and Baba some pocket money. I understand that Shabana blew it up instantly but Baba did not spend a penny, saying, 'I can smell Mummy's perfume in this.' Alice told me that for the month that I was away in Pakistan, Baba slept holding my blouse to his eyes. But my son is no pushover: Baba was four years old when Kaifi told him off about something and Baba insisted on giving an explanation. His father's anger rose a notch higher, 'Don't answer back! Keep quiet!' he reprimanded Baba, who looked Kaifi in the eye and muttered, 'God has given me a tongue to speak, so I will speak!' Baba likes to press his point home and will dispute endlessly to prove it. Often I get so exasperated that I give up saying, 'I think you should have been a public prosecutor!' Even though he loves a good argument Baba has always spoken in a very gentle manner. His voice is so pleasing that Kaifi called him 'Rasgulla' after the soft white milk dumpling soaked in syrup. As an adult and a very successful cinematographer he remains as gentle as he was as a child.

Baba has always had a marvelous sense of the comic and the absurd. He was just five, and we were visiting Hyderabad when all the children of the family got together to put on a variety show. Baba staggered on to the stage with a bottle in his hand and announced, 'I too shall act!' Acting drunk he stuttered and sang, *'Dife is a dweam, and in a dweam what is tlue and what ale lies?'* a song from the film *Jagte Raho*. He got a hearty round of applause from the audience and several pecks on his cheeks from me. That was perhaps the last time that he took centre stage. Baba has always been reticent and is uncomfortable in the limelight. He was about nine or ten when I discovered that he hero-worshipped Shammi Kapoor and loved to impersonate his dancing. I have always had two left feet and was thrilled to see that my son was such a fleet-footed dancer. He was happy to dance for me but would shy away from performing in company much as I would ask him to do so.

❦

I suspect that our move from Red Flag Hall to Juhu disrupted Baba's interest in formal schooling. After we were forced to pull him out of Hill Grange he changed several schools and found if difficult to settle into any particular one. Baba missed classes and played truant from the many schools Kaifi found for him but he remained an avid reader. He would lie in bed reading for hours on end and often drop off to sleep with an open book, but clearly, this was not sufficient to equip him for life.

When Baba was around seventeen Kaifi arranged for him to work as an Assistant Director on Chetan Anand's film *Hindustan Ki Kasam*, which was being shot in Delhi. One day Baba walked off the sets and came back to Bombay. He tried to give me an explanation for quitting work, 'The technicians are treated in a very unjust manner;

they do most of the work but they cannot even ask for an extra cup of tea, while people like us are free to waste as much food as we like. It is not possible to make a film without the technicians, and to be mean-spirited about their food is unacceptable.' I gave him an earful, 'If you refuse to work, how do you think you will survive? We are not going to live forever, how are you going to fend for yourself? You must work.' I think my tirade had some effect on him, because that night he went to see my nephew, the cinematographer Ishan Arya who was particularly attached to my children. Ishan offered Baba a job, asking him to report for work the following morning. It is because of his apprenticeship with Ishan that today Baba is the exceptional cinematographer that he is. Ishan was Baba's true guru and taught him not just camera technique and lighting but gave him useful tips on the importance of personal grooming. He advised Baba, 'Never forget to wash your hands with cologne after a meal because you have to get very close to the actor's face with your light meter to check the lighting.'

It was through Ishan that Baba met Bapu, a renowned South Indian director with whom Baba started his career as an independent cameraman. Bapu, who is an exceptional illustrator, impressed upon Baba how critical it is to frame a shot because the language of cinema is expressed primarily through images. Both Ishan and Bapu, masters of their art, had a formative influence on Baba's work.

⋈

Most of Baba's early work as a cameraman was in south India where people found it difficult to pronounce his name Ahmer Azmi. This was how, professionally too, he became Baba Azmi. Now the name Ahmer Azmi only appears on his passport and cheque book. Baba has worked on some great commercial and critical triumphs such as *Mr. India* (dir. Shekhar Kapoor, 1987) and *Tezaab* (dir. N. Chanda, 1988). As a cameraman he is especially sensitive to the words of actors who take great comfort in working with him because he can often anticipate an unrehearsed moment.

When Aamir Khan, who is a good friend of his, heard that Baba was directing his first music video based on Kaifi's poem, *Jab bhi choom leta hoon in haseen ankhon ko, sau chiragh andhere mein jhilmalane lagte hain* (When I kiss these enchanting eyes a hundred lamps begin to shimmer in the darkness) he volunteered to feature in it without charging a fee. Kaifi's poem is romantic and I was surprised to see that Baba has interpreted it politically and used the imagery of stark poverty as a metaphor for darkness. I could not but smile when he told me, 'For Abba, darkness meant the plight of the unfortunate and the poor.' All said and done, Baba is Kaifi's son. There was a time when Baba had no interest in art films and dismissed most of them as 'slow' and 'boring', but now that he is in the process of directing a film he has chosen a story about a photographer who goes back from the city to his village and organizes the villagers to raise their voice against exploitation. I can see glimpses of Kaifi's life in this story. Baba is very inspired by his father's life and says, 'I cannot work in the village like Abba, but I feel that if I am considerate towards people with whom I come into contact and can distinguish between right and wrong, then I believe I am following the trail blazed by Abba.'

৩৬

In 1984, during the shooting of *Pyari Behna* (dir. Bapu, 1985), Baba met Tanvi Kher, a terrific actress who was playing the title role. They decided to get married but Tanvi's parents, the famous actress Usha Kiranji and Dr Manohar Kher, were against the match because they were Hindu and Baba was a Muslim. Baba and Tanvi got married but her parents did not participate in the wedding ceremony. With time, Baba has won over members of her family so completely that now, Tanvi likes to joke that they love Baba more than they love her.

Tanvi has made a place for herself in our hearts. Kaifi called her Dulhan Pasha, which is an affectionate form of address for daughters-in-law in Hyderabad. She is warm and insightful and has adapted wonderfully to our way of life without losing her individuality. Tanvi has great style and runs a gracious home where Kaifi and I have always been at ease. In fact, Kaifi's poem *Doosra Banvas* (The Second Exile), which is about the riots that followed the demolition of the Babri Mosque, was written in Baba and Tanvi's home. I too, make frequent visits to their home, and although I have my own house in Janki Kutir, I enjoy staying over for a few days. I enjoy listening to them talk about their work. Over the years, what I have come to admire most in Tanvi, is her steadfastness. When I am sick or feeling low, she supports me like a rock.

I am fortunate that both my children care about the ideals that Kaifi lived for. I am happy that not only do I have good relationships with my children, but I can also see that both of them are extremely happy with their respective partners, for whom I feel a profound warmth and sympathy.

11

He was an Unusual Man

On the ill-fated night of 9th February 1973 we were struck by a tragedy that was to transform our lives. It was nine o'clock; Kaifi and I were sitting and chatting with Adil, Zakia and my nephew Ishan when the telephone rang. It was Yunus Pervez inviting Kaifi to a party at the film director S.M. Abbas's house, because a friend of his wanted to meet Kaifi. As Kaifi stood up from his chair he seemed unsteady on his feet. Worried I asked, 'Is everything all right?' He laughed, 'One look at my wife is enough to make me lose my balance.' I watched uneasily as Kaifi went off to Abbas's party.

At eleven o'clock that night the gate bell rang. I saw four men carrying Kaifi like a corpse and as they laid him down on his bed, I saw that his breathing was irregular. Kaifi moved his hand up to his head several times, as though he had a severe headache. Although I felt faint, I managed to say a silent prayer asking God to give me the strength to call Chetan Anand. Chetan Sahib arrived within minutes, bringing with him his brother-in-law Dr Madhok, who was a surgeon. 'It's nothing,' the doctor said, 'he's had too much to drink, and will be fine by morning.'

I had done some reading on homeopathy and said, 'But, Doctor Sahib, these symptoms look like those of a brain hemorrhage.'

'How can you speak like this about your husband?' Dr Madhok said in a censorious tone. He wrote a prescription and left. Chetan

Sahib rushed to Bandra and returned with the medicines, which were for a common cold. Baba returned home at around midnight and instinctively knew that his father had a serious illness that could have long-term consequences. He saw me weeping and hugged me, saying, 'Mummy, don't worry, Abba will be fine. I will go to the producers who owe him money and demand that they pay up.' I felt that in an instant Baba had grown up from a seventeen-year old boy to a twenty seven year old man. That night, Baba and I kept vigil.

At three o'clock in the dead of night I heard a thud and sat up in bed; Kaifi's left hand had dropped by his side like a log of wood. He was semi-conscious and asked, 'What was that?' I knew this was a stroke. I leaned across Kaifi, propped up his arm with mine, and pretending it was his I reassured him, 'See, Kaifi this is your arm.' At four in the morning Baba went to our family doctor's house, but his wife refused to disturb him, saying that he was not well. Baba refused to budge and eventually returned home with Dr Jain at nine o'clock in the morning, by which time some of Kaifi's friends had also arrived.

Umesh Mathur and Sathyu were with me when Dr Jain examined Kaifi and pronounced, 'He has had a stroke, but he will recover.' He wrote a prescription and was about to leave when the telephone rang. It was Rabab Jafri. Choking on my words I told her, 'Kaifi has had a stroke.' She informed Sardar Bhai, who sprang into action, 'Shaukat, bring Kaifi to Breach Candy hospital immediately; we shall have a room booked for him.' I was in a quandary because all we had was a hundred rupees which I had pledged for Kaifi's recovery and put under his pillow. A few minutes later Sultana Apa called, urging me to take Kaifi to the hospital, 'Moti, bring Kaifi immediately. If I arrange for an ambulance from here we shall lose precious time.' It was well past noon and Kaifi was drifting into a coma when Sathyu returned with an ambulance. At around one o'clock in the afternoon we arrived at Breach Candy Hospital where Sardar Bhai and Sultana Apa were waiting for us with two neurologists in attendance. The doctors informed us that the following seventy-two hours were critical. At four o'clock that evening Kaifi opened his eyes. All our friends from IPTA were standing around him and Gita Hattangadi rushed to me, 'Bhabi, quick, wash your face; Kaifi Sahib has regained consciousness.' I ran to Kaifi, 'Have you got a cardamom?' he asked. I took one out of my pouch and put it in his mouth.

Sultana Apa was standing by my side, 'Do you know who this is?' I asked cautiously.

'Yes, of course, this is Sultana,' he answered. Kaifi was beginning to lose consciousness and the doctor asked us to leave the room.

Shabana, who was in Saharanpur, left for Bombay the moment she heard of her father's illness. She arrived the following day, as Kaifi's friend, the documentary filmmaker Sukhdev had made arrangements for her to travel by air. As our house was miles away from the hospital, Sultana Apa and Sardar Bhai invited me to move in with them as they lived round the corner from Breach Candy. They were alert to all my needs. Every evening, they would accompany me to the hospital during visiting hours, between four and seven. Every time the telephone rang I rushed to it as though possessed. Sardar Bhai put an end to this and took charge of answering the telephone even when it interrupted his afternoon nap. I was inconsolable and wept incessantly. Sultana Apa counselled me, 'Moti, if your tears could make Kaifi well I would be the first one to say, "you must cry some more," but it is medical attention that will make him better, not your tears. All this weeping will certainly ruin your health when it is essential for you to remain strong to look after him.'

As Kaifi was in the intensive care unit the doctors' orders were that he was to have no visitors. However, the newspapers had reported his illness and there was a constant stream of well-wishers. Shabana and Baba posted themselves as sentinels on either side of the door to their father's room, and did not let anybody near him. Kaifi's visitors' list was long and spanned a vast social spectrum from government ministers to all the local gardeners from our neighbourhood in Janki Kutir. The latter would stand outside the ICU and pray to Bhagwan to restore the health of their Bhagwan-like Sahib. Of all his many friends, Muslim, Hindu and Sikh, there was not one who did not go to his or her mosque, temple or gurudwara to pray for him, and it was because of their prayers that Kaifi gradually recovered consciousness.

After a month in hospital Kaifi came home. Baba had gone to every producer for whom Kaifi had written songs and managed to recover some of the money they owed him, and this helped pay the hospital bill. Chetan Anand took care of part of the medical expenses and I borrowed some money from friends to engage a day nurse to help me look after Kaifi for a month. The stroke had affected Kaifi's left arm and leg. He was able to stand on his feet and walk with the help of a stick, his left arm was paralysed. Even though Kaifi knew I was always by his side he began to sink into a depression. At times he would ask me, 'Why don't you poison my tea?' At others, he would point to the rooftop opposite our window and say, 'If somebody aims at me from there, the bullet will hit me straight in my forehead and I will be free of this unbearable illness.'

On a friend's advice I took Kaifi to the ayurvedic hospital in Kottakal in Kerala, where their medical practice is quite unique. At the clinic the first thing they did was to shave Kaifi's head. Every day they made him sit in a tub full of oil, after which he was given a massage. Several times through the course of the day drops of ayurvedic medicine were put in his nose, and he was advised not to sit under the open sky. After a month in Kottakal we returned to Bombay, and while there was no improvement in Kaifi's paralyzed arm, he did come out of his depression.

ॐ

Mehdi was not just Kaifi's friend, but is like a member of our family. He was living in Delhi at the time, where he arranged an evening in Kaifi's honour. He invited P.C. Joshi and Begum Akhtar, the incomparable ghazal singer, whose voice I used to hear on the radio on my way to school as a little girl in Hyderabad. P.C. Joshi suggested that the Soviet Writers' Association should invite

Kaifi to Moscow for treatment. With the intervention of Suhasini Chattopadhyaya, who was Sarojini Naidu's sister and the first woman to join the Communist Party of India, Kaifi went to the Soviet Union. He was away for two months and we had very little contact with him. Phone calls were almost impossible and letters took an age to reach their destination. I was anxious that Kaifi was on his own but had to keep faith that he was receiving the best possible medical attention.

The premier of Shabana's first film *Ankur* was on the evening of 24th September 1974. That afternoon she was telling me how she longed for her Abba to be by her side, when the telephone rang and she answered it. The voice at the other end said, 'Chirya,'

'Abba!' Shabana shrieked with delight, 'where are you?' Kaifi told her he was calling from Delhi and had just arrived from Moscow. Wresting the receiver from her hand, I said, 'Kaifi, forget how tired you are and take the next flight to Bombay. Shabana's first film is premiering tonight.' How radiant Shabana looked when she walked into the Eros theatre with her parents by her side! Kaifi had the uncanny ability of turning up unexpectedly when he was most missed.

The two months in Russia saw an enormous improvement in Kaifi's health. Once again he started attending mushairas, for which we travelled together by train to the remotest corners of India. After his illness Kaifi's love of travel increased. Perhaps, he wanted proof for himself and for others that his spirit had not been defeated. It is a shame that scant attention is paid to the needs of the disabled in our country. It was rare to find a railway station that had a wheelchair ramp. I would hold my breath and pray when Kaifi had to walk up and down the steps at different stations with the help of his stick. Sardar Jafri would often say in jest, 'Kaifi has confronted his stroke with such audacity that I don't think this illness will have the nerve to strike down another poet!'

☙❧

Gradually, as Kaifi learnt to live with his illness he was able to travel with an attendant and it was no longer necessary for me to accompany him everywhere. In 1976 however, I readily agreed to go with him to an important peace conference in Patna where, not unusually, there were many people who admired him. We stayed very comfortably as guests in a comrade's house. The conference, which was a huge success, was attended by a hundred thousand kisans who had converged from nearby villages, carrying red flags. On our return we witnessed an amazing spectacle: Patna railway station was ablaze, with a hundred thousand kisans waving a hundred thousand red flags as they boarded their trains to return home.

Our platform was heaving with people. Four coolies were carrying Kaifi on a chair, and our young hostess who had come to see us off was walking by his side. I was walking on the other side, carrying my handbag in one hand and a tiffin carrier in the other. Quite suddenly I tripped and fell flat on my face. My bag went flying in one direction and the tiffin carrier in another. I was terrified, certain I was going to be crushed to death by the multitude when I saw a kisan wearing the red badge of the Communist Party spring to my defence like a guardian angel. As he began to whirl the long staff he was carrying, the crowd milling around us came to a halt. The coolies too, acted with great presence of mind and put Kaifi's chair down, while our young hostess leaned across him as a human shield. This combination of courage, quick thinking and action saved us from being crushed to death.

Later that year, Kaifi was tackling the stairs of his hotel in Lucknow when he sprained his foot and fell, fracturing his hipbone in three places. His friend Bhisham Kapoor, who was a reporter with *Blitz*, was with him and rushed him to the Lucknow Medical College Hospital. Bhisham Sahni telephoned to tell me about this. I lost no time and immediately took a flight from Bombay to Lucknow to be with Kaifi. In the hospital, I found Kaifi surrounded by doctors. He had tubes coming out of his nose and mouth and his intestines had stopped functioning because of the shock of the fall. I went up to him and whispered in his ear, 'Kaifi, I am here; there is no need to worry.' After about fifteen to twenty minutes, Dr Goyal, the orthopedic consultant said, 'Your presence has given him strength and slowly but surely he is improving. If his condition had persisted, we would have had to operate on him.' I was under a lot of stress and had asked Mehdi to join me. The doctors advised him that Kaifi should be kept in Lucknow, as it was not advisable to take him to Bombay in his medical condition. I could do little but agree. Kaifi was moved into a tiny room with an en-suite bathroom, a kitchen and a small courtyard. Dr Goyal set the bone with skilful precision, but Kaifi's skin was too sensitive for his broken left leg to be put into a plaster cast: it had to be kept in traction and he had to lie flat on his back for four months. I stayed with him throughout that time.

Kaifi was a man of extraordinary will power and did not yield to pain, but with the dawn of each new day he would say, 'Shaukat, thank goodness another day has passed.' Sometimes, he would ask, 'How will I ever be Sagar's pony again?' Kaifi loved Ishan's son, the three-year old Sagar who had made a habit of climbing on to his back. To cheer Kaifi up I hung photographs of Shabana, Baba and Sagar on the wall opposite his bed. Shabana came to see her father and was most distraught because she felt utterly powerless, 'Mummy, we can see Abba's pain but we cannot take away any of it nor can we share it.' To this day I marvel at Kaifi's resilience, because in those four months he never mentioned his pain and discomfort.

We were in Lucknow during Moharram. Kaifi's nurse would bring news of the Shi'a–Sunni riots as dead bodies of young boys were brought to the Medical College Hospital. Kaifi composed a ghazal from his hospital bed.

This is not Lucknow

We would shed tears not blood when we mourned
It must be some other place, for this is not Lucknow

They use knives more readily than tongues
This is not how Mir Anis and Atish would speak

Look at the blood dripping from the wounds of both sects
Friends, is it not the blood of Islam?

Give this carnage its true name
Because you've not been cleansed by blood

You believed you were robbing me of my wealth
But friends, it was your honour that you lost.

The flame you extinguished so senselessly
It was the light of hope.

1977

❦

Looking after Kaifi and coping with the stress of his illness had taken a toll on my health. In 1983 the Party decided to send both of us for treatment to the Soviet Union. In the hospital in Moscow we were given separate rooms, which caused me great anguish, although it was here that I was given a new lease of life. I had a lump in my left breast which, if left untouched, could have become cancerous. The Russian doctors operated upon me, removed the cyst and saved my life. The hospital staff and people around us were warm and compassionate, but I found the atmosphere quite dismal. The doctors were quite worried about my consistently high blood pressure. When matters became unbearable for me I went up to them and said, 'I spend the whole day stuck in my room in a towelling robe. No wonder my blood pressure shoots up. Please allow me to wear my own clothes and watch my blood pressure return to normal!' Mercifully, this made sense to them.

The following day a young man came up to me and asked in chaste Urdu, 'Are you Mrs Shaukat Kaifi?'

'Yes, indeed' I replied.

'I am your interpreter,' he said, 'and have come to take you to your hotel. You will be discharged from the hospital.'

'Really!' I shrieked with joy. I dashed off to my room, cast off the offending towelling robe and happily draped one of my beautiful saris. Kaifi and I went to the hotel where Munish, Mirza Ashfaq Beg and many of our other friends were gathered. I was overjoyed to hear from them that Faiz Ahmed Faiz was in Moscow and wanted to meet us. I dressed Kaifi up in a pristine white kurta, draped one of my finest saris, and we took off for Faiz's room. He had quit drinking at the time but we sat around drinking wine and listening to him reciting his poetry. After a long and pleasant evening when we returned to our hotel room we were informed that arrangements had been made for us to travel to Georgia for a holiday in a beautiful resort called Suchikatika. This cheered me up because I had heard that Georgian men are very handsome and the young women look like fairytale princesses. Indeed, a beautiful girl was Kaifi's interpreter and a handsome young man was mine. The next day we set off with our interpreters to a place which undoubtedly was heaven on earth.

The town had mountains on one side and the sea on the other. The beach was covered with flawless white stones the size of goose's eggs. For our diversion there were many board games such as chess, and if we wished we could always go to the theatre or the cinema. Each meal was a delicious spread of such variety and quantity that it was not possible for anyone to do justice to it. But human nature never fails to startle me; for despite our creature comforts and the astonishing beauty of the people and our surroundings, a deep sense of dissonance had set in, because nobody around us spoke our language. Kaifi had struck up a friendship with a comrade from Afghanistan who had come to Suchikatika for a change of air. I asked him if he had any cassettes of Urdu ghazals because I was longing to hear my language. He produced a tiny tape recorder and presented me an audiocassette of Urdu ghazals sung by a famous Afghan woman singer. Oh, the rapture, as I spent the entire day listening to the ghazals. Soon, engineered by me, we returned to India. Our long holiday in Russia and Georgia had acted as an elixir for both Kaifi and me. Everyone commented that I was looking at least ten years younger and the Bombay doctors confirmed that the Russian doctors had done well by me. Kaifi too, was looking good; his face had not had such a fresh glow in ages.

I travelled the world with Kaifi. Our travels would leave me physically drained but I was content to be with him. However, there were times when I found his behaviour really irksome. In 1994 we were invited to Dubai for the Kaifi Festival (*Jashn-e-Kaifi*) where Kaifi was to be presented a purse of seventy thousand rupees. Typically, Kaifi did not accept the money and asked instead for a video camera for IPTA. This irritated me because I wanted to buy a wrist watch and a gold chain. I kept my frustration to myself because I did not want to make Kaifi unhappy. Kaifi and I toured the United States on two occasions, visiting at least half the cities in the country. We had to put up with the tedium and the stress of staying in each city for two or three days, which meant that I was constantly packing and unpacking. To add to the fatigue of travelling were our personal chores. Kaifi's clothes were washed in a machine but the burden of ironing our high maintenance clothes fell upon me. The daily grind of bathing Kaifi, dressing him and taking him to mushairas wore me down and I resolved never to go to America again but Kaifi never gave in. He continued to attend mushairas whenever and wherever he was invited; I went to some and not to others. Gopal, who was Kaifi's attendant, accompanied him everywhere.

∞

When Shabana became a member of the Rajya Sabha, she was allocated a large bungalow in Delhi. She put a bedroom suite at our disposal and throughout Shabana's term as Member of Parliament, whenever Kaifi and I visited or passed through Delhi we stayed at her house. One day I was lying on my bed, reading while Kaifi was relaxing on the bed next to mine, when quite unexpectedly, Gopal walked in followed by two men carrying a large crate.

'Where should we put this?' asked the men.

Gopal responded, 'Here, thank you.'

I asked, 'What on earth is this?'

'It is an air conditioner,' Gopal said, 'the owner of Jet Airways Mr Naresh Goyal has sent it for Abba's computer class in Mijwan.' I looked at Kaifi in amazement and images of Mijwan as it was twenty years earlier began to roll before my eyes.

We are in Safdar Bhai's house.

SHAUKAT

(To Safdar Bhai) Safdar Bhai, where should I have a bath?

SAFDAR BHAI

Don't worry, Dulhan the electric supply hasn't been cut off for the day, so the tubewell should have plenty of water. I'll tie two sheets and create an enclosure for you to bathe.

I begin to soap myself when a gust of wind rises and the sheets begin to fly around.

SHAUKAT

(*Panic-stricken*) *Hai, hai,* don't come here! Please, please don't...

Haphazardly, somehow I finish my bath, get dressed and run from there.

An Indoor Scene: Day

There are guests in the house. There is no firewood. I gather all the fallen leaves in the courtyard with a broom; light a fire and place the kettle on it; I heat the water and serve tea.

An Outdoor Scene: Night

It is the dead of night and it is raining. There is no bathroom in the house and Kaifi needs to use the lavatory. Everyone is asleep. I'm trying to figure out where to place his mobile commode. I do not want to disturb all those who are asleep. I put the commode in the courtyard, take a lantern in one hand, and supporting Kaifi with the other, I bring him out to the courtyard. The rain falls fast and in sheets. I rush in, bring an umbrella and stand there holding it over Kaifi, getting drenched myself. There is rain and darkness on all sides, except for the flickering of a muted lantern.

Mijwan was a village frozen in time. It was as though Mijwan was waiting for Kaifi to come to its rescue. Kaifi started returning to his village regularly even though we no longer had a house there. At Partition, his family house had been usurped by some distant relative. Kaifi's cousin Safdar Bhai kindly invited us to treat his house as our own. This is where we would stay on our visits.

The first task Kaifi set himself was to get a road built from Mijwan to Phulpur. The farmers refused to part with an inch of their land, even though Kaifi took great pains to explain that the road would be useful for them to carry their produce to the market. There was a whispering campaign and some villagers began to ascribe personal motives to Kaifi. Never one to be deterred, Kaifi turned for help to V.P. Singh, the Chief Minister. I knew this was going to be a long haul and leaving Kaifi with his attendant, returned to Bombay. Some weeks later, I was told that a statue of Shankar Bhagwan had miraculously made an appearance at the exact spot that was marked for the road. V.P. Singh advised Kaifi to go back to Bombay fearing that the matter could turn into a Hindu–Muslim riot. 'Give it time,' he told Kaifi, 'I am sure the statue will return to where it came from.' It took many years and five changes of government before he could get the two kilometers of road between Mijwan and Phulpur completed and Kaifi would often remark, 'I wonder how Sher Shah Suri succeeded in constructing the Grand Trunk Road.'

Kaifi's next concern was to build a school. Finding land for the school was not easy either. The potters from the village had taken over all the government or zila parishad land to dry the cow-dung cakes which they used for fuel. Kaifi called one of them and told him firmly, 'Harilal, the land must be cleared by tomorrow.' Even though Harilal went away muttering under his breath the land was vacated. Some villagers started spreading rumours that 'Chacha is building this school for his own children.' Sita Ram, who looked after Kaifi's land, reasoned with them, 'Chacha's children have finished their education and live in the city. Why on earth would they want to study in a village school?' Some months later the same Harilal sidled up to Kaifi and said rather sheepishly, 'Chacha, every morning when my granddaughter is brushing her hair, she says with great pride, 'Dada, look, I too am going to school!' Today Kaifi's school is an intermediate college where young people, not just from Mijwan but also from neighbouring villages can get a decent education.

One day in the early eighties Kaifi said to me very gently, 'It's time to build our own house in Mijwan. How long can we go on living in someone else's house?' He handed me twenty five thousand rupees, which was all the money that he had. I have always been a city person and the idea of settling down in the village filled me with horror. But I knew that Kaifi had made up his mind and decided to take the line of least resistance. By now, Shabana had a very successful career in films, and she said, 'Mummy, please build the house exactly as my Abba wants it.' Within a year the house was ready for us to move in. Mijwan has a tiny population of barely fifty families. There were four other concrete houses, the rest were built with mud and had thatched roofs. It became a matter of some discussion in the village that Chachi had built a house with four bedrooms and three bathrooms. There was a constant stream of visitors, and the villagers would walk around the house exclaiming, 'Oh dear, oh dear, Kaifi Chacha's house has lavatory upon lavatory!' They would take turns to flush the water closet, and then run off giggling.

Kaifi had asked me to build a large hall where the villagers could watch television. They would arrive in droves and shriek in amazement, 'Look! Look! A man is walking inside the box!' The village children were rather scruffy and I thought of a novel way to encourage them to pay attention to their personal hygiene, and stipulated, 'Any child who wants to watch television will have to bathe and change into clean clothes before coming here.' Such was the allure of television that the children began to arrive all spruced up.

Kaifi decided to switch to the use of bio-gas for fuel and for a few days the villagers supplied us with cow-dung, but soon they started coming up with excuses. Kaifi understood that they too needed dung-cakes for fuel and bought a gas stove and a cylinder from Azamgarh. I had brought a pressure cooker from Delhi, and whenever the village women would hear the whistle, some of them would come rushing in and marvel, 'Why is the whistle blowing Chachi? Is a train about to arrive?' Pleased with their own joke they would rush off hiding their grins with the corner of their sari pallus. The people of Mijwan had never seen a pressure cooker, just as they had never seen a television. My world and theirs could not have been more removed from each other, but such was my pleasure in seeing Kaifi happy that I began to find contentment in the simplicity of village life.

DAYS AND NIGHTS IN THE VILLAGE

Mijwan Outdoor: Morning

It is five o'clock in the morning. I wake up to the tinkling of cowbells, which is sweet music to my ears. It is winter and farmers with tattered old pieces of cloth tied round their heads are driving their bullocks to their fields. People are sitting around fires warming themselves and I wrap myself against the cold. Gently, I wake Kaifi up.

SHAUKAT

(*Calls out*) 'Sita Ram, light a fire, we shall have tea on the lawn.'

Mijwan Outdoor: Morning

As far as the eye can see mustard fields have transformed Mijwan into a land of gold. It seems that a village belle has spread her gorgeous yellow dupatta across the horizon.

Mijwan Outdoor: Night

It is a moonlit night, the village is asleep and a deep silence casts a spell. Kaifi is nursing his drink reclining against a bolster. I ask him to recite a poem. He recites a ghazal.

Kaifi had written a ghazal on his village; it is a great pity that the poem is lost, but I recall the matla:

> *The scent of goodwill pervades this land of mine*
> *Love still lives in this land of mine.*

Mijwan Outdoor: Night

Fireflies are glowing in the dark. I decide to put on a much loved raga. Kaifi and
I lie on our beds under the sky counting the stars.

❧

In the morning I would go for a walk in the fields and gather mogra flowers in a basket. Upon my return I would find Kaifi waiting for me under the mango tree in our garden. I would arrange the flowers on the table and sit on the chair next to Kaifi's, waiting for Gopal to bring the trolley laden with tea and biscuits. Kaifi would watch with satisfaction as young girls in uniform walked past his gate to school. Often he would remark, 'How wonderful that young Shi'a girls who were not permitted to look out of their windows till yesterday are going to school now.' Every morning a group of old men would stroll in, looking forward to their cup of tea and more so the biscuits. One morning I served an old man his tea; unable to control his disappointment he exclaimed, '...and my biscuitva?' I noted his disappointed expression and said, 'Chacha, I am sorry we have run short. I shall send for some biscuits from Azamgarh.' I find the local Awadhi language very sweet and the practice of adding 'ia' or 'va' to word endings utterly charming. Thus, a motor car is a 'motoria' and a radio is a 'raidva'.

At around eleven o'clock, Shabbir Bhaiyya, Safdar Bhaiyya and Mehdi Bhaiyya would gather in our verandah. All three of them were distantly related to Kaifi and older than him. They were in their eighties, perhaps even older and were keen card players. As decks of cards were brought out, Kaifi would join them in a game of 'seven hands.' If for some reason, one of the brothers was missing they would summon me, saying, 'Dulhan, please join us, we are one short.' Always glad to join the card game I was astonished to discover that the old gentlemen were expert cardsharps and my darling husband was a few steps ahead of them! We would play cards until one o'clock and then disperse for lunch after which both Kaifi and I would take a nap.

From four o'clock onwards, a demanding schedule commenced for Kaifi, and we had a steady stream of visitors. Some days it was the District Magistrate and on others the Superintendent of Police. They would sit with Kaifi discussing the needs of his village or field his recommendations for jobs for people from his village. The district officers and the police authorities always tried to accommodate Kaifi's requests, but occasionally when they had to turn down something, they would do so by making polite excuses. Our very accomplished cook whom Kaifi had discovered in Barabanki would make the most delicious samosas and pakoras for our guests, and sweets were brought in from the halwai in Phulpur. The officers and their companions rarely touched anything; however, the two jeep-loads of soldiers accompanying them ate heartily.

Late in the evening, burqah clad women would gather in my room and we would talk about this, that and the other or watch television until dinner time. Our house would glow in the darkness of the village because our generator ensured a constant supply of electricity.

ॐ

It was 1990 and the school had now been running successfully for four years. Kaifi was cheered by its success and wanted to take it up to the matriculation level. Around the same time Mulayam Singh, who was the Chief Minister of U.P., announced that he would visit the village and honour Shabana with the Avadh Ratna because she had received the International Human Rights' Award, along with Mother Theresa, from President Mitterrand of France. A day was fixed for the Chief Minister's visit and Mulayam Singh arrived in a helicopter with the Governor, Motilal Vohra. The villagers had never seen a helicopter and could not take their eyes off it. I had become accustomed to entertaining dignitaries in the village and laid out an elaborate dinner set with matching glassware. I adorned the house with the best rugs and linen from my collection. Cooks were brought in from Azamgarh, but the Chief Minister and the Governor Sahib arrived late that afternoon and neither of them ate a morsel. While the villagers had a feast, the chief guests drank tea from my tea set and then came on to the stage.

A dais had been constructed in the school ground and the village girls sang songs of welcome in Awadhi. Mulayam Singh made a speech, saying how pleased he was to see the development of the village. In her speech Shabana said, 'We have a long list of things that we can ask for but our greatest need is to upgrade the girls' school, taking it up to matriculation. And the next step is a degree college for girls, because the nearest college is forty kilometers away in Azamgarh. And for all this we need the government's help.' Mulayam Singh stood up immediately and pledged twenty lakh rupees, saying, 'My government is bound to ask me, "Why did you give so much money?" But I am ready to face the consequences.' The villagers were delirious with joy and Kaifi's happiness was boundless. Sadly those twenty lakh rupees did not come Mijwan's way, because I fell ill and Kaifi had to return to Bombay with me. Taking advantage of Kaifi's absence, people from the neighbouring village of Ambari got their hands on the money.

Kaifi did not lose hope and when we returned to Mijwan he sent for our driver and car from Bombay. Kaifi now travelled around the state, meeting various officials, working ceaselessly for his village. He had no qualms in using his abundant charm and talent to win over reluctant officials. The Congress politician Mohsina Kidwai told me that when she was Minister for Telecommunications, Kaifi had charmed her into sanctioning telephone links to Mijwan by writing his request in verse. Similarly, cutting across miles of red tape, Kaifi persuaded the Director General of the Post and Telegraph department of the need for a sub-Post Office in Mijwan, on the strength of a poem he had written as an official application. Runa Bannerjee, who had set up SEWA (Self Employed Women's Association) in Lucknow, told me that she thought she was hallucinating when she saw the legendary Kaifi Azmi outside her office sitting in his car, which he refused to leave saying, 'I will not budge from here till you promise me that you will send a trainer to my village to teach the girls chikan embroidery; they need to find employment.' Runa was overwhelmed, and she set about making arrangements for two of her teachers to go to Mijwan. Now the village girls are in a position to earn twelve to fifteen hundred rupees a month, working under the aegis of the Mijwan Welfare Society, which Kaifi had set up on his own land. Today it runs with support from Home of Hope Inc., an NGO that is based in San Jose. Its founder, Dr Nilima Sabarwal, is one of the most selfless women I know.

It was Kaifi's way that the moment he had accomplished one task he moved on to the next. One day he said to me in his usual quiet manner, 'I am going to open a computer class here, so that my children will have better employment opportunities.'

I laughed out loud and said, 'Here? Where electricity is only available for two to three hours every second or third day?' Kaifi remained silent, but then he was not a man given to conversation. I was in Bombay when I heard that rooms for the computer class had been constructed with a donation from Mr Amar Singh, the leader of the Samajwadi Party who had given seven lakhs from his Parliamentary funds. Shabana paid for ten computers from her Parliamentary quota. Through Kaifi's efforts teachers were found for the computer centre. Naresh Goyal, who is a very close friend of Shabana and Jadu's, loved and admired Kaifi and was happily roped in to provide an air conditioner. Kaifi had already bought a generator to ensure an uninterrupted supply of electricity for the computer centre.

When I saw the men carrying the air-conditioner into our room countless memories came rushing back to me. My heart went out to my tenacious Kaifi who had refused to be crushed by his physical frailty and had brought his village from medieval times into the twenty-first century. Contrite that I had scoffed at his intention to make a computer centre, I turned towards Kaifi and saluting his courage, kissed his forehead.

∞

The villagers were beginning to think of Kaifi as the person whose magic wand was a panacea for all their needs. One day, instead of going to their local M.P., a group of agitated locals turned up with a petition at Kaifi's doorstep. The only railway station for miles was Phoolpur Khorasan Road. This was on a narrow gauge line that connected the people of Mijwan to the district towns of Shahganj and Azamgarh and from there to Benares. The government in its wisdom decided that there was no use for this station and issued an order for it to be pulled down. The villagers informed Kaifi that the police was thrashing up the young men who were demonstrating against the demolition, and that his friend Hari Mandir Panday was badly injured. Kaifi knew that the railway was the villagers' lifeline and he was outraged. He rushed to the railway station and positioned his wheel chair in the middle of the train track. The Station Master had no choice but to give orders for the work to be stopped. The policemen too were forced to put an end to their brutality.

Kaifi's next step was to go to Delhi to meet Jaffar Sharif who was the Railways Minister. Kaifi said to him, 'Your heartless policemen have thrashed the young men from my village. I am carrying with me a bloodstained shirt. Do you want to see it?' Jaffar Sharif Sahib was visibly upset and said, 'No. Please... I do not need to see it. I shall pass an immediate order that the Phoolpur line be reinstated.' Kaifi returned triumphant, carrying the order with him and the villagers danced with joy. Other than Kaifi I was the only person privy to the fact that there was no shirt in his brief case, and his threat was merely a ploy to intimidate the Minister. The narrow gauge line was soon reinstated.

Emboldened Kaifi now demanded that this link be converted into a broad gauge line. He lobbied Ram Vilas Paswan who was the new Railways Minister and was successful in getting this done. But Kaifi did not rest till he got a third Minister, Nitish Kumar to start a train service between Azamgarh and Bombay. The Godaan Express is a daily train service, named after the famous Hindi writer Premchand's novel *Godaan*. Taking up from where her father left, Shabana lobbied the government during her term as Member of Parliament to start a train between Delhi and Azamgarh: now there is a daily train called Kaifiyaat Express, named after the collection of Kaifi's poetry. A third train between Kolkata and Azamgarh is to commence soon. All these trains stop at Khorasan Road Station and the people of Mijwan are linked to the world in ways they could perhaps only have dreamed of.

∞

Nobody really knows the correct date of Kaifi's birth, but one day his friend Sukhdev decided that Kaifi was born on 14 January, and from that day onwards this was deemed to be his birthday. I remember 14 January 2002 particularly well because Shabana came to Mijwan to celebrate her father's birthday. Whenever Shabana came to the village people poured in from neighbouring villages to petition her about their problems. This occasion was no different and from the early hours of the morning people had surrounded Shabana: somebody wanted a job; somebody wanted a transfer and somebody else wanted a road constructed. It was four o'clock in the afternoon and Shabana who had not eaten a morsel was sitting in the verandah listening to the people's problems. Kaifi, who was watching all this, lifted himself out of his bed and asked me, 'Please, may I have some money?'

'Why?' I quizzed him.

'Don't ask questions and just give me some money,' he said, as I handed him a hundred rupees. Kaifi called his driver and set off with Gopal. Nobody knew where he was going and nobody had the nerve to ask. He returned after an hour and called Shabana into his room, 'My little Chirya, my villagers have tired you out. Look, I have had your favourite samosas freshly made for you. Eat them while they are still hot! You can deal with the villagers later.' Shabana was delighted and devoured all the samosas, perhaps, sparing one for Kaifi. This was the last time that Kaifi was able to leave his bed on his own.

A week later Kaifi's health took a turn for the worse. He was finding it very difficult to breathe. I knew that his condition was serious. Shabana was filming in Goa, so I telephoned Baba and Jadu in a panic. Jadu calmed me down, 'Shaukat Apa, don't worry, leave everything to us. Baba and I shall make all the arrangements. If you want Kaifi Sahib to be admitted into a hospital in Benares I can make arrangements from here but if you would prefer to take him to Delhi, that too, can be arranged.' The following day Baba arrived in Mijwan with Parna, Shabana's dearest friend who is like a daughter to me. Parna who has seen us through good and bad times did not tell Baba that her arm was fractured and was in a cast. She travelled from Bombay to Mijwan with her broken arm hidden in her shirt sleeve.

Kaifi's condition was critical. The District Magistrate had made immediate arrangements for an ambulance to be sent from Azamgarh, to take Kaifi to Benares. When we saw the vehicle we were shocked. It was so filthy that Parna, Baba and Gopal had to wash it clean with antiseptic before we could risk putting Kaifi on the stretcher and set off for the three-hour journey from Mijwan to Benares. The road was full of potholes and every time the ambulance would jolt my heart went out to Kaifi but he did not complain. At Varanasi (the official name for Benares, which is also called Kashi) airport, typically there were no arrangements for disabled passengers. Baba carried his father up to the aircraft and made him sit in his seat. It struck me that this time too, Baba was there to help just as he had been thirty years earlier. I prayed throughout the seemingly unending one-hour flight. At Delhi airport, Dr Naresh Trehan had arranged for an ambulance to meet us and we went to Escorts Hospital where Kaifi was kept in intensive care for a month. I was drained of all energy and could not bring myself to go to the hospital every day. Shabana, who was back from Goa, had to attend Parliament and Baba had to get back to Bombay for a shoot. Tanvi, who is from a family of doctors, flew in to Delhi and took charge. For several weeks she sat outside the ICU from morning to evening, and was there for Kaifi as she would have been for her own father. When his condition stabilized Shabana and Baba decided to move their father to Bombay.

∝∞

In March 2002 Gujarat was ravaged by communal carnage. Home all day, Kaifi would lie in bed watching television, his eyes full of pain. He had fought against communalism all his life and was deeply hurt to witness this orgy of violence. I was so horrified by the events in Gujarat that I could not bear to read the newspaper and kept trying to switch off the television. On 1st March 2002 Shabana had gone to Ahmedabad with Amar Singh, Raj Babbar and Sitaram Yechury. They spoke with Narendra Modi, the Chief Minister of Gujarat over the telephone but were not allowed to visit the riot-affected areas. Narendra Modi forced all four of them to return to Delhi, saying, 'Everything is under control; these are just minor law and order incidents.' The following day more than twenty-five people were burnt alive in Naroda Patia, a suburb of Ahmedabad. Shabana returned to Bombay broken-hearted and related her experience to Kaifi who embraced her, saying, 'Do not lose heart, and carry on with your work. One day this madness will stop.' I stood silently at the door and watched them share their grief.

Kaifi was at home for less than a month before he had another severe attack of asthma, and almost went into a coma. As always, I called Baba in the middle of the night and he rushed to my side. Baba took Kaifi to the Jaslok hospital where he was kept in the Intensive Care Unit for forty-eight days with some of the best doctors of Bombay attending to him. It was around this time that the Sahitiya Akademi honoured Kaifi for his services to literature, conferring on him the

Sahitya Akademi Fellowship, its highest award. Many esteemed literary personalities came from Delhi to grace the occasion but Kaifi could not attend the ceremony and received the award in hospital. Forty-eight days is a long time to be in intensive care, isolated from friends and family but Kaifi never uttered a word of complaint.

I remember the day I entered the ICU and saw Kaifi lying with his eyes shut. I was deeply saddened to see a hint of tears in the corner of his eyes. Rarely had I seen Kaifi cry, not even on the death of his brother or his first born. Baba was equally upset to see his father in this state, and tried to comfort him, 'Abba, the doctors have given permission to move you out of the ICU. Your friends will be able to visit you and you can also watch the news on television from tomorrow.' But Kaifi did not open his eyes. There was a commotion outside the ICU because the Chief Minister had come to see Kaifi, but he did not open his eyes. I whispered in his ear, 'Kaifi, the Chief Minister Vilasrao Deshmukh is here to see you.' Kaifi's eyes remained closed but he smiled weakly and held out his right hand, which the Chief Minister took warmly into his own and said a few words of comfort. After the CM's departure I asked Doctor H. G. Desai 'Doctor Sahib, isn't this a sign of a depression? Should Kaifi be given some medicine for this?' The doctor smiled and answered, 'No medicine. All he needs is company. Tomorrow we will move him to another room and all will be well.'

I found little comfort in the doctor's words and an unknown fear gripped me. I felt as though somebody had squeezed my heart. I kissed Kaifi on his forehead and said, 'Kaifi, from tomorrow you will be allowed visitors and all your friends will come to see you. You will have a TV and I shall visit you every day. Don't lose hope.' He remained silent and did not open his eyes. The following morning Baba arrived at the hospital at eight o'clock and moved his Abba from intensive care into a new room. Baba did not like this room and decided to shift Kaifi into a larger room that had been vacated. I am told that Kaifi did not open his eyes. I phoned Baba to ask him if I could come to the hospital and he said, 'Mummy, Abba has been moved from one room to another and he is exhausted. Let him rest today; visit him tomorrow.' I agreed, even though my heart was telling me that all was not well.

Early the next morning the telephone rang at six o'clock. When I answered it there was silence at the other end of the line. I said, 'Hello, hello' several times but the silence persisted and I put the receiver down. After a while the telephone rang for the second time, 'Hello, hello,' I said, and yet again there was silence. I reprimanded the silent caller, 'If you don't have anything to say, why do you keep calling?' I slammed the receiver back into the cradle. It was the nurse, Maria, who was making the call, as she held the receiver to Kaifi's ear in the hope that the sound of my voice would revive him. How was I to know that this was my Kaifi making his last phone call to me? Like a light that begins to flicker and grow dim, Kaifi too, began to fade away. Finally, at six o'clock on the morning of 10th May 2002, Kaifi left me forever.

∞

The memory of that day stings me like a poisonous snake. Baba comes into my room and says, 'Mummy, Abba has been laid in his room. Will you see him?' I am not sure how, but I manage to say, 'Yes, I want to see him.' I enter Kaifi's room with faltering steps but a heart that continues to beat and eyes that remain dry. I stare at him; I stare at a lifeless man with whom I have spent fifty-five years. There are thirteen days left for the fifty-five years to be complete—from 23rd May 1947 to 10th May 2002. Countless questions start spinning around my mind, 'Is this the same person for whom I was willing to give up my life? Is this the person who was my life? Will he never speak to me again? Will people soon come and take him away from me forever?' I find it difficult to stand and return to my room where I lie down trying to face the bitter reality. The poisonous snake tightens its grip on my neck and continues to sting me.

∞

Kaifi was not just an ideal husband, he was my friend who encouraged me to be independent and never imposed his will on me. He always respected my opinions, my wishes and my desires. In fact, he took great pleasure in my success and wanted me to achieve fame as an artist. It was not easy for Kaifi to live in the village without me but he never complained because he had an extraordinary ability to withstand hardship. I went to the village when I wanted to, and when I had had enough, I returned to Bombay. I am convinced that my absence exacerbated his illness.

Kaifi adored his children and his relationship with them was that of a friend. If they faltered he did not lose his temper but tried to reason with them. He would go to great lengths to make them happy. Shabana loves mangoes but when she was a little girl the fruit was rarely seen at our table because it was rather expensive. One day, Shabana brought two dozen mangoes from her friend Parna's house, and happily told me, 'Mummy, these mangoes came from Parna's village and her Mummy has sent them for us.' Kaifi noted his daughter's remark, and though he did not say a word he filed it away in a corner of his heart. Many years later when Kaifi started living in his village after his illness, one of his first projects was to hire a truck and go to Malihabad. He brought back three hundred mango saplings and planted a small mango orchard, so that his daughter would always have her heart's fill of mangoes. Every year Kaifi's man Friday brings mangoes for Shabana from Mijwan.

Kaifi was not given to demonstrating his love for his son but he was delighted to see Baba's first interview as a cameraman in the newspaper. He cut it out, had it framed and hung it on the wall opposite his desk. Baba and Kaifi had a very strong bond and often sat together in silence for hours.

Kaifi had a cavalier attitude towards his health and never let his illness stand in his way. He had a chronic cough and though the doctor had forbidden him to have anything cold, Kaifi always drank cold water. He ate and drank wherever he found himself and this, too, contributed to his ill health. I would call the doctor and give him his medicines, after which he would gain a new lease on life, but oblivious to his illness he would continue working.

Kaifi cared for working people and the destitute, and had a firm belief in communism. He always carried his Party membership card in his briefcase, and would often take it out, saying with great pride, 'This is my most precious capital.' The objective of his life was to change the world, to banish poverty, hunger and ignorance. But he understood that to change the whole world would take a very long time, so he turned instead to answer the call of his village, where he did indeed achieve a huge transformation. Kaifi's love for his village was obsessive. Even so, Kaifi would have approved of Baba and Shabana's decision to give his cherished collection of over five thousand books, many of which are rare, to the Aligarh University Library, because many more students can have access to them.

Kaifi had created the Mijwan Welfare Society and built its offices on his own land. He had ceiling fans installed in every room. That night all four fans were stolen and there was mayhem in the village. I was really angry and raised my voice loud enough for all to hear, 'I don't understand why Kaifi wants to kill himself working for such ungrateful people.' Kaifi remained silent. Shabana, who is more impatient than her father, asked him, 'Abba don't you get frustrated when the change you are struggling for doesn't occur at the pace you'd like it to?' Kaifi answered her with equanimity, 'Betey, when you are working for change, you should build into your expectation the possibility that the change might not occur within your lifetime, but if you carry on regardless, change will come, even if it does so after you are gone. Then, how can there be room for frustration?'

Kaifi was a grand human being. I have never seen a more gracious man. When asked, 'Kaifi, how are you?' He would always smile and say, 'First class.' This was so even a few days before he died. It is true that he always remained first class.

I do not think there could be a more befitting epitaph for Kaifi than Jadu's poem.

He Was an Unusual Man

He was an unusual man
He was a melody of love; he was a rebel's song
At times he was fire, at other times a flower
He was an unusual man
To the poor he would say
Bad times can pass away
To the tyrants he would say
The gold crowns on your heads
Can one day melt away
To rules he would say
I can break you
To comforts he would say
I can forsake you
To the winds he would say
I can turn you
To a dream he would say
I'll make you come true
To hopes he would say
I am your companion
I'll walk with you, however arduous the journey
I'll never tire
To life he would say
I'll adorn you
Ask me for the moon
I'll bring the moon to you
To people he would say
You must love humanity
You must save the earth
It is wasting away
He was an unusual man

To all obstacles he would say
I'll triumph over you
One day, all trace of you will be erased
The world will forget you
But my story stands apart
In eyes that have dreams in them
In hearts that have hope in them
In arms with strength in them
On lips with words on them
I'll live after I fade away

He was an unusual man.

Javed Akhtar
Mumbai
20 July 2002

Epilogue

Each morning a new day dawns and there is birdsong; sometimes clouds gather and raindrops drift into the verandah. Like every other day our housekeeper Vinod arrives with the tea and puts the tray down before me, but the chair facing me is empty. It is not occupied by my Kaifi who would walk to the garden despite his frail condition and sit in the chair opposite mine, waiting for me to pour out his tea. He would reach out for his cup with trembling hands and look at me in companionship, drinking his tea as though it were ambrosia. These were the most cherished moments of my day. It was under the spell of one such moment that Kaifi composed a poem.

A Moment

Life is the name of a few moments
And among them that single moment
In which two eyes speak as they
Look up from a cup of tea
And descend into the heart
They descend into the heart, and say
Today, you must not speak a word
Today, I shall not speak a word
Just sit as we are
Holding hand in hand

Holding the gift of pain
Holding the warmth of feelings
For who knows, at this very moment
Far away upon a mountain, the snow begins to melt.

In 1947 before we were married and Kaifi was staying at our house in Aurangabad, I had given him a slip of paper on which I had scribbled, 'With you by my side life will pass by like the morning breeze caressing flowers.' I am amazed how quickly these fifty-five years have passed. My heart is unfulfilled. I wish Kaifi had stayed with me longer.

⚭

Life carries on as usual Kaifi, but you are nowhere to be found. When you went to the village I was secure in the knowledge that you would return. I recall a New Year's night when the house was full of revelry. I was rushing around looking after the guests when without warning a little wish awakened in a corner of my heart, 'What if Kaifi were here?' How amazed I was to see you walk through the gate, leaning on your stick. I ran to you and wrapped my arms around you, 'Arrey vah! How come you're here? How did you know that your absence was the only thing that was keeping me from feeling happy? How wonderful to have you back. Now that you are here my New Year will begin.' How did you suddenly turn up that night? Kaifi, will it never be possible for you to return unannounced and for me to lose myself in your arms? I know this will never be. I shall have to accept the truth that you have gone away to a far off place from where no one returns. Why does this happen? When will this burden on my heart be lifted? For how long will I have to go on living without you? They say people like you do not die, they live forever, but when will I believe this Kaifi?

Glossary

Abbajan	term of endearment and respect for father (lit. Abba: father; jan: life).
Agar	a fragrant wood, *Aquillaria agallocha*, used for incense and perfume.
A'la Hazarat	His Eminence (lit. exalted presence).
Alu ka bhurta	mashed potatoes with Indian spices.
Ammajan	term of endearment and respect for mother (lit. Amma: mother; jan: life).
Apa	older sister.
Atar	perfume.
Attaar	perfumerers.
Baji	older sister.
Bare Bhaijan:	term of endearment and respect for older brother. In this context Senior older brother. (lit. Bare: big; Bhai: brother; jan: life).
Bari Apajan	term of endearment and respect used for older sister. In this context, Senior older sister. (lit. Bari: senior; Apa: older sister; jan: life).
Bari	gifts from the groom's family for the bride consisting of clothes and jewelry.
Beta/Betey	affectionate usage for child. (lit. beta: son).

	Perhaps, this was so as it was not the done thing to refer to gender; especially for girls.
Bhabi	brother's wife.
Bagharay baingan	aubergine filled with finely ground and prepared spices and steamed.
Bhai	brother.
Biryani	layers of rice and meat prepared with special spices, and steamed with saffron.
Burqah	the outer garment worn by women in order to veil themselves.
Chacha	paternal uncle; father's younger brother.
Chadar	a piece of cloth for a woman to cover herself with (lit. sheet).
Chandni	white sheets spread on the floor for people to sit on. (lit. moonlight).
Charpai/charpoy	a local bed strung with rope. (lit. four legs).
Chauki	a low seat or a pedestal; also a small enclosure.
Chawl	a tenement.
Chikan	a refined white thread embroidery, done with mainly shadow work and drawn thread work. Lucknow *chikan* is famous throughout the world.
Choli	woman's tight fitting bodice.
Chote Bhaijan	term of endearment for older brother. In this context, Junior older brother. (lit. Chote: small; Bhai: brother; jan: life).
Choti Apajan	term of endearment used for older sister. In this context, junior older sister. (lit. Choti: small; Apa: older sister; jan: life).
Dada	paternal grandfather.
Diwali	one of the most important of Hindu festivals, signaling the return of the god Rama from

	fourteen years of exile in the forests. People light up their homes, pray and celebrate.
Dulhan	(*lit. bride*). In Urdu and Hindi speaking cultures it is customary to call the daughter-in-law *Dulhan* or *Bahu*.
Dupatta	veil.
Eid	A Muslim festival. There are two main Eids in the Islamic calendar. Eid-ul-Fitr to mark the end of Ramdadan and and Eid-ul-Adha, which follows after two months and ten days.
Gharara	flared pantaloons, cut elaborately, on the cross and worn by Muslim women, particularly in UP.
Ghazal	a lyrical and metaphysical love poem of rhyming couplets, with strict conventions for rhyme and metre. The rhyme scheme is: aa, ba, ca and so on; and a ghazal must scan to the same metre. Originally used in India in the Persian language, it gained literary prominence and popular appeal through the Urdu language.
Ghee	clarified butter.
Gota	gold braid.
Gur ke Mithe chaval	sweet rice with raw cane compound.
Hafiz	one who commits the Holy Qur'an to memory (lit. custodian).
Hannafi al Mazhab	a Sunni Muslim (lit. Hannafi sect), from one of the four main Sunni Muslim doctrinal schools.
Harijan	term used for untouchables, coined by Gandhiji. (lit. God's children).
Hemuru	a fine, much coveted silk brocade, which was a speciality of Hyderabad.

Holi	a Hindu spring season, on the last festival of colour celebrated at the end of the winter full moon day of the lunar month Phalguna (February/March)
Jharu	a broom.
Joray	a set of Hyderabadi bangles encrusted with sparkling semi-precious stones. (lit. a pair).
Juhi	jasmin.
Karga	cotton net with embroidery, described in text.
Kamatan	char lady.
Karchob	dense raised gold or silver thread embroidery which gives the effect being embossed.
Karhi gosht	meat curry cooked with yoghurt and gram flour.
Karhi mahi	meat curry cooked with yoghurt and gram flour, using fish spices.
Kathal	Indian breadfruit or jackfruit tree; *Artocarpus integrifolia.*
Kamdani	stiff gold or silver flat thread embroidery, in which each stitch is a dot that combines with other dots to make geometric or other intricate patterns. It is also called *badla* and *mukesh.*
Kebab	meat pounded or minced, marinated with special spices and grilled.
Kevra	name of a plant which has very fragrant flowers; the essence of which is extremely popular all over South Asia. *Pandannus odoratissimus.*
Khara dupatta	an ensemble of clothes, consisting of a *churidar pyjama, kurta,* and an *dupatta.* The latter two are usually made of net.
Khas	a fragrant grass; *Andrapogan muricattum;* the tattis are made from the roots. *Khas attar* is used particularly in summer months.

Khasdan	a small silver dish with a cover on which *paan gilohri* are served, impaled on silver sticks. Usually it is round and has a dome shaped lid. Often intricately worked with filigree.
Khichri	combination of rice and lentils; consequently the English kedgeree.
Kulche	a round, flat bread made with milk, flour and butter.
Kulfi	Indian ice cream made with specially reduced milk and pistachio, perfected in Lucknow.
Kurta	a shirt made up of two central panels, with side panels cut on the cross; it has two pieces, in the underarms to connect both sleeves to the garment and a front opening with a band for buttonholes.
Marsiya	an elegy or a lamentation; in this context, chanted particularly to commemorate the martyrdom of Husain, the grandson of the Prophet Muhammad.
Masnavi	a long poem in rhyming couplets with a rhyme shceme aa, bb, cc.
Matla	the first couplet of a ghazal
Maulvi	honorific used for a man well versed in Islamic scholarship.
Mirchon ka khatta salan	curry of chillies prepared with sour spices.
Misra	a hemistich; a single line of a poem.
Motia	single jasmine flowers.
Mogra	Double jasmin *or Jasminum zambac;* also called Tuscan jasmin.
Mushaira	an assembly of poets where they recite their poetry.

Nauroz	Persian new-year.
Nazm	a poem, with no fixed rules of form, metre or rhyme.
Nila totha	a poison.
Nihari	meat cooked all night to be served in the morning for breakfast.
Nikah	formal exchange of Muslim marital contract. (lit. to marry).
Pandan	silver boxes with containers that to hold all the ingredients required for the preparation of paan. Lucknow *pandan* are traditionally round, whereas Hyderabadi *pandan* a rectangular.
Pankha	fan.
Pau	a unit of weight measure, where four *pau* make a seer. Two seer are equivalent to a pound in weight.
Payam	message.
Phupi	paternal Aunt, father's sister, also called Phuppo and Bua.
Pipal	long pepper tree; *Piper longum.*
Pirhi	a low seat, with or without a back.
Purdah	the tradition and practice of women veiling and concealing themselves (lit. curtain).
Qaliya	meat, usually lamb, cooked with potatoes in thin gravy.
Qorma	chicken or lamb cooked with gravy prepared with special spices.
Rat ki Rani	flowering bush that gives out a fragrance at night. (lit. Queen of the night).
Razakar	as part of the Nizam's efforts to secure Dominion status for his State he enlisted the

	help of Muslim para-military volunteers, called the razakars. In 1948 the Nizam and the razakar were defeated by the Indian army and Hyderabad was merged into the Indian Union.
Rubai	quatrain.
Sahib	Sir.
Salim Shahi	hand-made pointed leather shoes, densely embroidered with gold or silver thread.
Shalwar	flared pantaloons ruched at the ankles.
Shervani	a long fitted, gentleman's frock coat.
Sarkar	master/mistress.
Shikram	a carriage drawn by an animal and called by this name in Hyderabad.
Taj	Crown.
Tamatar ka kat	a tomato ragout with spices.
Tarannum	reciting poetry as song.
Tola	a weight of 16 (in theory) and 12 (in practice) *mashas*, specially of gold or silver. It is more than an ounce.
Tonga	horse drawn carriage.
Vah	a term of applause like 'wow' but not slang.
Zari	strictly speaking gold thread for embroidery or weaving. *Real zari* at the time was real gold or silver thread. Now copper and nylon are also used to make *zari* like thread.

Zamindes

the garden concealed in the bud